Plants of the Bible

And

Their Uses

OTHER PUBLICATIONS

BOTANICAL SYMBOLS IN WORLD RELIGIONS - A Guide, Pittsburgh, 2001, 70 pp., illustrated, (ISBN 0-929699-12-2). A selection of botanical symbols used by Judaism, Christianity, Islam, Buddhism, Hinduism, Confucianism, and Taoism.

THE HEALING PAST *Pharmaceuticals in the Biblical and Rabbinic World,* edited with Walter Jacob, E.J.Brill, Leiden, 1993, 126 pp., (ISBN 90 04 09643 4), presents the papers of our international symposium on ancient medicine in Egypt, Israel, Mesopotamia, and early Rabbinic Judaism. Published as part of *Studies in Ancient Medicine.*

FLORA in *The Anchor Bible Dictionary*, with Walter Jacob, Vol. 2, Doubleday, New York and London, 1992.

BIBLICAL PLANTS *A Guide to the Rodef Shalom Biblical Botanical Garden*, Pittsburgh, 1989, 60 pp., illustrated, (ISBN 0-929699-01-7). This guide describes the Biblical plants Plant names are given in English, Hebrew, German, French and Italian.

FORGOTTEN IMMIGRANTS, *Plant Immigrants to Israel through Three Thousand Years*, with Walter Jacob, Pittsburgh, 1988, 23 pp. A selection of plants introduced to Israel in each century.

PAPYRUS, A Journal published during each of the summer months, edited by Irene Jacob, illustrated, 1990-2002.

GARDENS OF NORTH AMERICA AND HAWAII, *A Traveler's Guide*, with Walter Jacob, Timber Press, Portland, 1985, 367 pp., (ISBN 0-88192-017-7). Describes over 1400 public gardens.

PLANTS OF THE BIBLE

AND

THEIR USES

by

Irene Jacob

Rodef Shalom Biblical Botanical Garden
Rodef Shalom Press

Published by the
Rodef Shalom Press
4905 5th Avenue
Pittsburgh, PA 15213
2003

Library of Congress Catalogue Card Number 2001 130828

Jacob, Irene (1928-)

ISBN 0-929699-14-9

Cover photograph - pomegranate flower

CONTENTS

DEDICATION

For Walter in gratitude for his advice, encouragement and unfailing help.

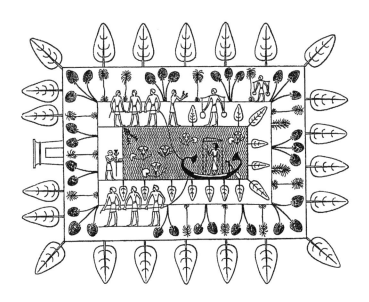

Garden. Thebes.

ACKNOWLEDGMENT

Research for this book began many years ago and I am grateful for contacts with various individuals who have been helpful. The pictures in this book have come from many sources, mostly nineteenth and early twentieth century studies and we are grateful to those anonymous artists. All profits from this printing will go to the Rodef Shalom Biblical Botanical Garden, for whose support I am grateful. My special thanks to Nancy Berkowitz for her suggestions which improved the text and her help with copy-editing. Last, but not least, my gratitude to my husband, Walter Jacob.

Scribes. Thebes.

INTRODUCTION

The Middle East has produced more than religions, wars, pyramids, and pharaohs. It was the site of perhaps the most significant economic revolution in human history. Here the first known human settlements in which farming was practiced were established. Among the many botanical gifts of the Middle East are wheat, which permitted the rise of the great Mesopotamian and Egyptian cultures, as well as European civilization – also barley, onions, dates, olives, figs, and other plants.

This book is designed to increase the enjoyment and knowledge of plants mentioned in the Bible and to provide a link between plants, people, and events of ancient Israel and the surrounding cultures.

Reading the Hebrew Bible and the New Testament, one is amazed at the role that plants play in them. The Bible mentions more than 110 plants, which are found in almost every book. Some occur only once, as the onion; others, like the vine, more than three hundred times.

More than 1,000 years of oral transmission preceded the written text of the Hebrew Bible. Biblical scholars of earlier generations were not botanists, so their translations and interpretations have little scientific value but remain historically important.

The psalms, along with the prophetic books, often refer to vegetation. Many parables, similes, and metaphors were drawn from the realm of agriculture. The frequency of a reference, however, does not necessarily provide an idea of the economic importance of a plant.

All descriptions of plant life in the Bible are casual, so many common plants known to have grown there have not been mentioned. A common species such as the Carob tree (described as "pods" in Luke 15:16) must undoubtedly have been cultivated in biblical times, but it is not mentioned.

Many people in the United States, and most people in the western world today, do not live close to the land. In third world countries, however, just as in biblical times, people are aware of the vegetation that provides their food, clothing, shelter, and medicine. Detailed descriptions were not necessary for the biblical writer, or for that matter, for the modern peasant.

RESEARCH OF BIBLICAL FLORA

Levinus Lemmens, in 1566, was the first to write a book that dealt entirely with the plants mentioned in Scriptures. Lemmens, however, had never visited the Holy Land. The great eighteenth-century Swedish botanist Carl Linnaeus (1707–1778) suggested that Palestine be studied to test his notion that specific plants are limited to a particular place. He was convinced that many plants were limited to certain parts of the world, a commonplace idea for us but revolutionary two and a half centuries ago. With the universal interest in the Bible, he felt that an exploration of Palestine would provide a good test.

Two of his pupils, Fredrik Hasselquist, in 1777, and Pier Försskål, were the earliest botanists who actually went to the Holy Land. They gave the world a first-hand, scientific description of the plants and animals then growing in the land of the Bible.

In the nineteenth century Napoleon's expedition to the Middle East sparked an interest in the flora of Palestine. Napoleon was accompanied by an entourage of scientists that explored Egypt and the surrounding countries even though the expedition failed.

4

Among the pioneers of the nineteenth century was Aaron Aaronsohn. Later modern research was carried out by Alexander Eig (1894–1938), who founded the botanical garden of the Hebrew University in the 1920s, and Michael Zohary, author of *Flora Palestina*.

CLIMATE

One might ask how it is possible for such a small country as the Holy Land, the size of Vermont and New Hampshire, to have so many plants. This is due to the diversity of the land, its climatic differences ranging from temperate in the north to subtropical and arid in the south. There are two seasons, summer and winter; spring and fall are seldom mentioned in the Bible. Rain, drought, heat, and cold figure in the Bible as the central themes in poetry, sermons, curses, and blessings. In a rainless region (no rain in any region from May to November), dew is important. There are on the average 250 annual dewy nights. Hunger and famine, the most feared disasters, are mentioned over one hundred times in the Bible.

GEOGRAPHY

The Holy land has been divided into five regions; the coastal plains, the central hills, the Rift valley, the plateau of Transjordan, and the desert. The topography is extremely varied. Altitudes range from Mount Hermon's 9,240 feet in the north to the Dead Sea's 1,306 feet below sea level.

PLANTS

The plants are listed in brief chapters that deal with the most important practical subdivisions of biblical plants. Their uses both in the ancient Near East and in modern times are listed. Because the medicinal uses are extensive, only a few of them are listed. Further information may be found in James A. Duke, *Medicinal Plants of the Bible,* as well as several foreign language studies.

HOW TO USE THIS BOOK

The plants are organized into categories most appropriate for ancient Israel. The English name is followed by the scientific designation and the area in which the plant originated.

A description follows, along with some comments on the plant in ancient times. The uses of the plant in ancient and modern times indicate the importance of the plant.

A single biblical verse has been selected for each plant. This is followed by the name of the plant in (H)–Hebrew, (G)–German, (F)–French, and (I)–Italian, which should facilitate identification in those languages.

Growing these plants in North America is possible in specific zones or by taking the less hardy plants indoors. Pertinent cultivation material has been included.

The accompanying pictures of daily life mainly show scenes of ancient Egypt as little material from Israel or the other ancient lands exists. Whenever possible the place and approximate dates have been provided

A source of plants as well as a selected bibliography are provided in the last section of the book.

This book should help the reader enjoy the Bible from a different perspective and encourage some to recreate a portion of that plant world in a home or display garden.

Forests, mentioned more than thirty-five times in the Bible, covered the hills of ancient Israel, but large trees for construction had to be imported, not only to Israel, but also to Egypt. Isolated, lowland trees could be viewed as part of the pagan worship denounced by the prophets. Fruit trees were especially important, since dried fruit provided food in time of famine; olives and grapes were an essential daily food for all economic classes.

ACACIA Acacia raddiana Leguminosae Mediterranean

Many references to *shittim* occur in the Bible, either to the tree or to designate the locality in which it was found. Four varieties are found in Sinai, and it is a common tree of the Judean desert. There are about 420 species in this genus. Some have supplied gum.

A. raddiana has a chestnut-colored, twisted trunk. It is a flat-topped, drought-resistant tree with low-lying, prickly branches and small compound leaves. Each leaf splits into six pairs on each side of its stem, each leaf splitting again into 5–12 additional pairs of leaves. The yellow, globular flowers are followed by brown, twisted pods.

There is no way to verify the age of acacias: they do not develop the yearly rings by which age is measured in other species.

ANCIENT AND MODERN USES

Wood: Strong, elastic, resistant to rot and fungal attack. The portable Tent of Meeting in the desert, as well as the furniture in it, was constructed of this hard timber. Clamps on mummy coffins, fuel, hand tools, posts. **Bark:** Tanning leather. **Bark Fiber:** Ropes. **Young Fiber:** Toothbrushes, chew-sticks. **Foliage, Flower, Fruit:** Fodder. **Flower:** Honey, garlands.

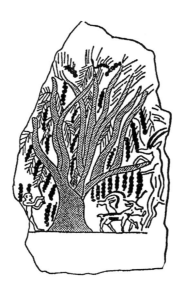

Acacia with twisted pods.

And thou shalt make an altar...of ACACIA WOOD. Exodus 30:1

H: Shita. F: Acacia. G: Akazie. I: Acazia.

CULTIVATION

Zones 8–11. Well-drained soil in full sun. Propagation by seed. The hard-coated seeds remain viable for 30 years and should be heated and soaked before planting.

ALLEPO PINE, JERUSALEM PINE   Pinus halepensis
Pinaceae
Mediterranean

Allepo pine stands remain on the Carmel, although the identification of the biblical *brosh* could also refer to "fir." It is considered an emblem of nobility and is named for a region bordering northern Syria and Turkey.

A fast-growing, drought-resistant monoecious evergreen up to 80 feet, with a shallow root system and rich in resins. The spreading lower branches die back when overshadowed by the upper branches. It is often used as a wind-break. Its leaves are twisted and two-needled. Male cones are long; female cones, ovoid and reddish-brown when ripe.

ANCIENT AND MODERN USES
Wood: Coarse grained and resinous. Used in Solomon's temple for floorings, doors, and ceilings; later, for boxes, railway sleepers, telegraph poles, charcoal. Also for shipbuilding and musical instruments. **Bark:** Tanning. **Stem:** Source of Greek turpentine. **Resin:** Embalming. Used for flavoring the Greek wines *retsina* and *roditys.* **Rosin:** Violinists' prime.

As for the stork, the FIR-TREES are her house. Psalms 104:17

H: Brosh Oren.   F: Pin d'Alep.   G: Aleppokiefer.   I: Pino d'Aleppo.

CULTIVATION
Zones 7–10. Resistant to dry conditions. Well-drained soil Propagation by grafting.

ALMOND   Prunus dulcis (formerly P. amygdalus)
Rosaceae
Mediterranean

Almonds are among the first trees to flower in spring. The Hebrew word means "diligence," and the flowers symbolize the awakening of spring. They are mentioned six times in the Bible. Another name for almond–*Luz*–is a place name. Almonds were found in the Negev and throughout the land. It is one of the earliest fruit trees domesticated in the Old World. Aaron's staff was an almond branch that budded overnight. Nuts were a suitable present for Pharaoh.

This spreading tree, growing to 20 feet, has a dark gray bark. Oblong leaves appear after the white or pink flowers have bloomed. The fruit is flat, furry, and, when dry, splits to release a weak-shelled stone that holds the almond kernel. Trees produce fruit after 5–6 years.

ANCIENT AND MODERN USES
Wood: Handle for walking sticks in Egypt (18th Dynasty). **Bark:** Gum similar to and used as a substitute for tragacanth. **Nut:** Food, marzipan, oil for flavoring. **Cosmetic:** Charred shells–may have been used for kohl soot (ancient Egyptian eye paint), perfume. **Medicinal:** Oil: emollient, mild laxative; Milk: lowers fevers; flour used in dietetic foodstuffs. In modern times in

California the shells are burned to produce electricity. **Symbolic:** Its flower may have been used for the design of the cups of the seven-branched lamp-stand of the desert tabernacle.

Painting the eyes with kohl. Wall painting in a tomb. Egypt.

Carry down the man a present, a little balm, and a little honey, spicery and ladanum, nuts and ALMONDS. Genesis 43:11

H: Shaked. F: Amandier. G: Mandel. I: Mandorlo.

CULTIVATION
Zones 6–9. Two varieties needed to produce fruit as they do not self-fertilize. Deep, well-drained, salt-free soil. Propagation by grafting or from seed.

APRICOT Prunus armeniaca Rosaceae
China

Many biblical scholars believe that the apricot or the quince, not the apple, was the first fruit mentioned in the Bible. Although domesticated apple trees are now found in Israel, wild specimens are not believed to have grown there in biblical times. Apricots, native to China, were probably introduced

11

early to Israel, where they are now abundant. Apricots in Cyprus are still known as "golden apples."

The tree has a reddish bark and grows to 30 feet. Pink or white flowers appear before its ovate leaves. Its fruit is subglobose, yellow with reddish cheeks.

ANCIENT AND MODERN USES

Wood: Firewood, drinking cups in Tibet. **Fruit:** Food, fresh or dried, alcoholic beverage *(Eau de Noyaux).* **Seed:** Substitute for almond oil. **Cosmetic:** Oil used in soap and perfume. **Medicinal:** Fruit high in vitamin A, antiseptic. Seed has ingredient marketed as "Laetrile," controversial agent for cancer control. Poisonous if chewed for an extended period.

But of the TREE of knowledge of good and evil, thou shalt not eat of it.... Genesis 2:17

H: Mishmesh. F: Abricotier. G: Aprikose. I: Albicocco.

CULTIVATION
Zones 5–10. Moist, well-drained soil. Feed with high-nitrogen fertilizer. Propagation by seed or by grafting.

BAY LAUREL   Laurus nobilis   Lauraceae
Mediterranean

Some biblical scholars believe that the "green bay tree" refers to the bay laurel, also known as sweet bay; it grows on rocky hillsides throughout the Mediterranean countries. The Romans named it from the word *laudare,* to praise, for it was thought to be worthy of the highest honors.

A slow-growing evergreen tree or shrub to 40 feet. Leaves are oblong, fragrant, leathery, with wavy edges. Yellow male and female flowers are borne on separate trees. Fruits in fall, produces a red-blue berry that contains an oily seed.

ANCIENT AND MODERN USES

Wood: Marqueterie work. **Leaves:** Dried–spice, wreaths. **Fruit:** Oil: Flavoring of some liqueurs. **Cosmetic:** Soap ingredient, perfumery. **Medicinal:** Leaf, berry: stomachic, astringent, and carminative, used for rheumatism and gout.

I have seen the wicked in great power, and spreading himself like a green BAY tree. Psalms 37:35

H: Ar. F: Laurier franc. G: Edle lorbeer. I: Lauro poetico.

CULTIVATION
Zones 7–10. Sheltered position and well-drained soil. Sun to part shade. Propagation by seed in fall or cuttings in summer.

BOX **Buxus sempervirens Buxaceae**
Mediterranean

The box tree is mentioned three times in the Bible and grows in the Galilee hills.

This is a hardy, long-lived evergreen growing to 20 feet. The trunk may be 12 inches thick. Leaves are thick and leathery, green above and paler below. Yellow flowers are followed by a papery capsule fruit with small, black seeds.

ANCIENT AND MODERN USES
Wood: Heavy and fine textured and as durable as brass. One of the densest woods, it barely floats in water. Statuary, wood-cut printing. Engraving plates, molds for casting —no other timber holds detail so faithfully. Flutes, clarinets which produce soft resonant much sought after tones. Writing tables, tobacco pipes, combs, spoons, mathematical instruments, inlay for ivory in cabinet work, chessmen, cork-screws, tool handles, shuttles, croquet mallets. **Cosmetic**: Leaf: Tannin, mixed with lye produces hair dye, dried and powdered provides shiny coats for horses

The glory of Lebanon shall come unto thee, the fir tree, the pine tree, and the BOX together.... Isaiah 60:13

H: Te'ashshur. F: Buis. G: Buchsbaum. I: Bosso.

CULTIVATION
Zones 3–9. Most soils; desires a sunny location. Propagation by cuttings.

BRAMBLE, BLACKBERRY   Rubus sanguineus
Rosaceae
Mediterranean

Thorny and prickly plants are often mentioned in the Bible. The blackberry is one of the candidates mentioned in the verse below.

A climbing plant with a cluster of radiating canes, erect at first, then arching downward. Leaves are hairy, with three to five leaflets. Flowers are white, followed by fruit: black drupelets on older shoots.

ANCIENT AND MODERN USES
Fruit: Food, juice. **Young Shoot:** Salad. **Medicinal:** Leaf, Root: Tannin used as astringent and as tonic for dysentery, diarrhea. Leaf chewed for bleeding gums, burns. Flower and Fruit: Remedy for venomous bites.

Then all the trees said to the BRAMBLE, "Come you, and reign over us." Judges 9:14

H: Petal Kadosh, Atad. F: Ronce. G: Brombeerstrauch. I: Rovo.

CULTIVATION
Zones 3–9. Moist, well-drained, fertile soil in sun. Propagation by cuttings, suckers, or seeds.

CAPER BUSH Capparis spinosa Capparaceae
Mediterranean

The Hebrew word for "desire" is identified by scholars with this plant. This may seem to be a far-fetched conclusion, yet the caper berry does have a stimulating effect, so describes man's old age, exciting his appetite.

A spiny shrub with thick leaves that spreads over rocks much like ivy. The flowers are white or pinkish, open in the evening and wilt by morning. The many-seeded berry hangs on long stalks.

ANCIENT AND MODERN USES
Unopened Flower Bud: Pickled as capers. (A good substitute is green nasturtium seed.) **Young Fruit:** Ancient aphrodisiac.

The almond tree blossoms, the grasshopper drags itself along and DESIRE fails: because man goes to his eternal home.... Ecclesiastes 12:5

H: *Zalaf Kosani, Abiyona.* F: *Câprier.* G: *Kapper.* I: *Cappero,*

CULTIVATION
Zones 8–12. Needs long, hot summers and full sun with good drainage. Propagated from fresh seed or semi-ripe cuttings.

16

CAROB Ceratonia siliqua Leguminosae
Mediterranean

The pods of the carob or locust tree were the "husks" of Jesus' parable of the prodigal son. Some biblical scholars believe that the "locust" eaten by John the Baptist were not insects, but were the fruit of this tree. Although it is found in many regions of the country it is not mentioned in the Old Testament, but is mentioned in the New Testament, Mishnah, and Talmud.

A long-lived, round headed tree to 40 feet high with glossy pinnate leaves and clustered spikes of small greenish flowers in spring and fall. The fruit, a sword-shaped pod, is tough, sweet, dark brown, rich in sugar and protein. Eight-hundred pods can be harvested from a single tree each season.

ANCIENT AND MODERN USES

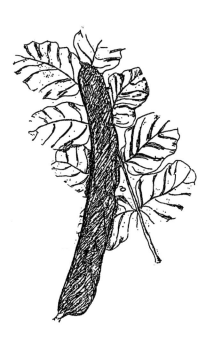

Wood: Easily worked. Turnery and cabinetry, fuel–charcoal. **Pod:** Processed to cocoa–like flour, candy. Source of alcohol. Fodder. In Cyprus molasses made from beans called *pasteli*. **Flour:** Dog biscuits, flavoring for uncured tobacco. **Seed:** Roasted–substitute for coffee–Carob coffee. Weights in ancient times. **Seed Gum:** Used in ice cream, salad dressing, pharmaceutical cosmetic products, detergent, paint, ink, shoe polish, adhesives, sizing for textiles, photographic papers, insecticide, match heads, tanning. **Medicinal:** Fruit: Catarrhal infections.

And he would gladly have fed on the PODS that the swine ate; and no one gave him anything. Luke 15:16

*H: Haruv.   F: Caroubier.   G: Johannisbrotbaum.
I: Carrubbio.*

Carob tree. Tomb of Mena, Thebes. 18th Dynasty.

CULTIVATION
Zones 9–11. Hot dry summers. Sun or light shade. Well-drained soil. As some plants bear only male or female flowers, interplanting of both sexes necessary for fruiting. Pods harvested before winter rains. Propagate seed in fall. Fruits after six years.

CASTOR OIL TREE Ricinus communis Euphorbiaceae
Tropical Africa

The huge leaves of the castor-oil plant is said to be the plant that shaded Jonah; other translations call it a gourd. Seeds have been found in a 5,000-year-old Egyptian tomb. It grows wild in Israel.

This tropical shrub may reach 15 feet. The hollow green, red, or violet stems become woody with age. Palmate leaves have veins usually the color of the stem. Male yellow and female pink flowers are arranged in racemes and lack petals. The fruit is a three-celled capsule covered with prickles. Each capsule contains three smooth, mottled, poisonous seeds.

ANCIENT AND MODERN USES

Seed: (Seed capsule contains most of the poison). Is 55% oil. Small seeds richer in oil than large ones. Egyptians used oil for lighting. Used in the chemical industry, as an aviation lubricant (has a low freezing point), in plastic, nylon, imitation leather, laundry detergent, necklace, typewriter ink; for dyeing cotton "turkey red"; component of rubber, celluloid, waterproof preparations, sebacic acid for candles, varnish, fly-paper; ingredient for restoring paintings. South Africans mix castor oil with kerosene as a culicide that prevents flies from attacking camels. **Stem:** Paper, wallboard. **Cosmetic:** Seed: Transparent nonfragrant soap; Egyptians blended it with fat to stimulate luxurious hair growth; base for unguents. **Medicinal:** Seed: after heat treatments: Oil: Science of serum therapeutics based on Paul Ehrlich's experiments with castor oil bean seeds. Egyptians used it as poultice for headaches, mosquito repellant. Contraceptive jellies, creams for ophthalmic preparations, antifungal agent, laxative. In Africa often used as means for infanticide.

And the Lord God appointed a PLANT, and made it come over Jonah.... Jonah 4:6

H: Kikayon. F: Ricin. G: Rizinusbaum. I: Risino.

CULTIVATION Zones 9–11. Sun, fertile-humusy, well-drained soil. Propagation by seed.

CEDAR OF LEBANON Cedrus libani Pinaceae
Mediterranean

Cedars of Lebanon were used by King Solomon to build the temple in Jerusalem. Although stone was used for the main construction of the temple, Cedars of Lebanon provided timber for the beams, paneling, columns, floors, and doors. The large timbers were floated 200 miles down the coast from Lebanon to Jaffa and hauled another 25 miles overland to Jerusalem, requiring 183,000 men to do so and seven years to build the temple These trees were also used for the construction of Solomon's own house and the House of the Forest of Lebanon, which greatly impressed the Queen of Sheba. In exchange, Solomon gave to Hiram, King of Tyre, 20 cities and annual deliveries of corn and oil.

Cutting wood for export. Karnak 19th dynasty.

The Cedar of Lebanon is mentioned over 70 times in the Bible. It was seen by the ancients as the king of trees and was imported from the 1st Dynasty to Egypt. The word *cedar* is derived from the Arabic *cedra,* meaning strength.

In more modern times, the Turks (1517–1918) cut huge numbers of trees. During WW I the allied armies used cedar wood for rails that ran from Palestine to Syria and for fuel. In 1963, the United Nations supported a program to add cedars to the

Joiners making fine furniture from timbers.

400 trees still in Lebanon. Seeds were germinated in Britain using German containers and French fertilizers under American automatic sprinklers.

The tree, with its dark gray trunk, may grow to 100 feet. With age (up to 3,000 years), the pyramidal form of this evergreen tree changes to widespread branches. The bluish-green needles are short, and the catkins of male flowers shed golden pollen. The female cones are oval, green, and ripen in two years.

ANCIENT AND MODERN USES

Wood: Free of knots, durable, fragrant, takes a fine finish, and is fungus resistant. Houses, bridges, shingles, paving blocks, boats, railway sleepers, garden furniture, funerary articles, veneers, and chariots. Plugs in recorder mouthpieces (resistant to saliva). **Cosmetic:** Oil, Perfume. **Rosin Oil:** Protection of manuscripts, embalming (to destroy intestines). **Medicinal:** Oil from cones and wood: In biblical times used to cleanse lepers.

Found on Lebanese postage stamps, flags, and coins.

The righteous shall flourish like the palm tree: he shall grow like a CEDAR OF LEBANON. Psalm 92:12

H: Etz Halebanon. F: Cèdre du Liban. G: Libanonzeder. I: Cedro del Libano.

CULTIVATION

Zones 6–9. Well-drained soil and full sun. Propagation from cuttings, layering, or grafting.

C YPRESS Cupressus sempervirens Pinaceae Mediterranean

Although there is some confusion as to which Hebrew word refers to this tree, *brosh* is mentioned 20 times in the Old Testament. The cypress is native to the Land of Israel. It was one of the trees Solomon used to build the temple in Jerusalem. Today, natural stands of the tree grow in Gilead, Edom, and southern Sinai. Cypress is often grown in cemeteries. In Bethar it was a custom that when a boy was born, a cedar tree was planted, when a girl, a cypress. The Romans planted groves of cypress because it was profitable for poles for wedding canopies: this is why it was called a daughter's dowry. Named after the Island of Cyprus, where the tree was worshiped.

An evergreen that grows to 80 feet and can live to 500 years. The small, aromatic, scalelike leaves are resinous. Male cones are terminal, yellow-brown. Female cones are ovoid, brown or grayish, and ripen in the second year. The cypress is an earth healer: Attached to its feeding roots are tiny nitrogenous nodules which improve the soil.

ANCIENT AND MODERN USES
Tree: Windbreak. **Wood:** Red to yellow brown, fragrant and insect resistant. Construction, shipbuilding, mummy cases, ancient idols, furniture, lances, musical instruments, doors (the doors of St. Peter's church in Rome, built of cypress wood 1,200 years ago, show no signs of decay. The cypress gates of Constantinople stood for over 1,000 years). **Cosmetic:** Oil: Perfume, providing ambergris and labdanum-like odors. **Medicinal:** Antiseptic. Cones: Pulverized, were used for wounds. A decoction of the same drunk for diabetes and rheumatism.

Carpeter making chairs. Thebes.

Hiram, King of Tyre, had furnished Solomon cedar trees and CYPRESS trees.... I Kings 9:11

H: Brosh. F: Cyprès commun. G: Zypresse. I: Cipresso commune.

CULTIVATION
Zones 8–10. Full sun, well-drained soil. Propagation by seed
or cuttings.

DATE PALM Phoenix dactylifera Palmaceae
Mediterranean

Its place of origin has never been satisfactorily determined. It
is known to have grown abundantly in the region between the
Euphrates and the Nile.

One of the oldest cultivated trees, it may be the tree of life of
the Bible. Mentioned 48 times from the first to the last book of
the Old Testament. Jericho was known as "the city of palm
trees." Palms in Israel and Egypt often provided landmarks.
Palm leaves are among the three species that constitute the
Lulav for the Feast of *Sukkot.* Palms are symbolic of peace
and plenty, grace and elegance. Its Hebrew name *Tamar* is
still a popular women's name, an allusion to graceful carriage.

This palm, to 100 feet, has large, feathery leaves that may
open to 20 feet. Plants are unisexual. Date palms are wind
pollinated, but to increase the yield, the fruit is set by artificial
pollination—cutting of cream-colored male flower branches
and fixing them among the female whitish flower bunches.
Only one male tree need be planted to pollinate 100 females.
The fruit is oblong, with a hard stone grooved down one side.
Palms begin to bear when 5–8 years old and average about
150 pounds per tree annually. Arabs say that "its head should
be in fire (sunshine) and its feet in water."

Small garden at a grave with date palms. A stele in Cairo.

Monkeys assisting in gathering fruit. Beni Hassan.

ANCIENT AND MODERN USES

A Persian hymn to the Date Palm includes 360 uses. **Trunk:** Fences, rafts, fuel, pipes, small bridges. **Leaf:** Roof thatch, hung on walls for insulation. Motif for ornaments of King Solomon's temple, emblem of victory on coins. **Young Leaf:** Cooked and eaten as vegetable, brooms. **Leaflet:** Woven into mats, baskets, utensils, sails, roof thatch, when combined with ground peanut shells and corn cobs used to make insulating boards. **Fiber:** Ropes. **Fiber from Base of Leaf:** Egyptian wigs, ropes, matting, baskets. Mixed with camel hair and made into cloth for caravan tents. **Leafless Midrib:** Sticks, cages, chairs, doors, palm-stick torches. **Unopened Flower Spathes:** When pierced believed to be the "strong drink" mentioned in the Bible as distinct from wine. **Fruit:** Food—fresh or dried, paste, jam. Made into honey (it is over 60%

New date wine poured into jars.

25

sugar). Bees are mentioned four times in the Bible, honey, 49 times. Some Arab tribes subsist for months on dates and milk only. **Bruised Fruit:** Arrack. **Fermented Fruit:** Wine (also used in embalming for rinsing body cavities), vinegar, ingredient for beer (makes beer less intoxicating). **Unripe Green Fruit:** Dye, tanning. **Crown:** Sap used for wine, syrup. **Seed:** Animal fodder (when soaked and ground, especially toothless camels), necklaces, oil. In India roasted and ground, used to adulterate coffee. **Finely Ground Seeds:** Flour. **Medicinal:** Ingredient for cough medicine, laxative.

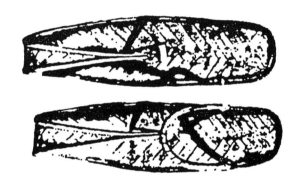

Palm leaf sandals.

The righteous shall flourish like the PALM tree.... Psalms 92:13

H: Tamar.   F: Dattier.   G: Dattelpalme.   I: Palma da datteri.

CULTIVATION
Zones 10–12. Poor soil if given good drainage in sun or part shade. Needs male and female flowers for pollination. Propagation from seed in spring or by taking lateral branches from the base of the palm.

E BONY Diospyros ebenum Ebenaceae
India, Sri Lanka

A luxury wood imported since ancient times.

Tall, slow-growing evergreen tree, with a smooth bark. The heartwood makes it valuable. The small, bell-shaped pink unisexual flowers with rolled-back petals are followed by fleshy berries. This species is the only one which gives a black heart wood without streaks or markings.

ANCIENT AND MODERN USES
Wood: Hard and brittle. Difficult to work but has an excellent finish. Used for inlay, together with ivory or box. Furniture, sculpture, handles, door knobs, butts of billiard cues, cups, veneers. Musical instruments, violin fittings, organ stops, castanets and black keys of keyboard instruments. In China: Chopsticks, pipes, carved stands, vases. **Medicinal:** Believed to be antidote for poison in ancient times.

The men of Rhodes traded with you; many coastlands were your own special markets, they brought you in payment ivory tusks and EBONY. Ezekiel 27:15

H: Hovenim. F: Ébeniér. G: Ebenholzbaum. I: Diospiro ebano.

CULTIVATION
Zone 9–11. Well-drained soil with ample water in the growing season. Propagated from seed or by layering.

E TROG Citrus medica Rutaceae
Asia, Arabia

Not native to Palestine but believed to be the first of its genus to grow there. By 200 B.C.E. it was interpreted as the "goodly tree," whose fruit is used during the Jewish festival of Sukkot.

A small evergreen tree with short spines and leathery leaves. The flowers are white inside and purplish outside. The yellow, thick-skinned, giant lemon is fragrant and bitter.

ANCIENT AND MODERN USES
Fruit: One of the four species at Feast of *Sukkot.* For this purpose, it must have its pistil intact to be *kasher* and is used together with the *lulav.* Combined with quince seeds, cloves, lemon, and sugar and made into a jam. **Peel:** Candied. **Cosmetic:** Perfumes. **Medicinal:** Peel: Oil, distilled from the peel, is used as snakebite antidote.

And ye shall take you on the first day the fruit of the GOODLY TREES.... Leviticus 23:40

H: Etrog.   F: Cédrat.   G: Zitrone.   I: Cedro.

CULTIVATION
Zones 9–11. Well-drained, friable, slightly acid soil, full sun. Needs regular watering and feeding with nitrogen and potassium. Propagation by grafting.

FIG   Ficus carica   Moraceae
Mediterranean

Figs are the first fruits mentioned in the Bible, with more than 70 references, from the third chapter in Genesis to the sixth chapter of Revelation. The importance and value of the fig to the Israelites is illustrated very graphically by the fact that whenever the prophets censured the people for their wickedness, they threated that the vine and fig crops would be destroyed, and when they wanted to extend the promise of great reward they said that the vine and fig crops would be restored. Four different Hebrew words are used in the Old Testament, referring to the tree, fruit, unripe fruit, and cakes of dried figs.

They are among the seven species listed in Deuteronomy and have been found among tomb offerings in dynastic Egypt. In biblical imagery the fig tree symbolizes prosperity and peace.

A shallow-rooted deciduous tree to 30 feet, with palmately lobed leaves and wavy margins. The flowers are borne inside the fruit. Pollination is by the female fig wasp, which crawls through a small hole to reach the flowers.

The purple, greenish-yellow fruit ripens in 80–100 days, with 30 to 1,600 small seeds per fruit. The stem, leaves, and fruit have a milky latex obtained from wounded tissue.

Harvesting figs. Grave of Chnumhotep.

ANCIENT AND MODERN USES
Fruit: Food, fresh or dried, made into cakes, wine, jam, paste, candies. Still used in bakery product—Fig Newton.® Flavoring for liqueurs and tobacco. The Assyrians used it as a sweetener. From it can be isolated a protein-digesting enzyme "ficin" for tenderizing meat. **Seed Oil:** Used as lubricant. **Leaf:** Fodder in India, baskets, dishes, umbrellas. Fig leaves are still used by sculptors on their statues. **Cosmetic:** Source of woody odor in French perfume *feuille de figuier absolut.* **Latex:** Used in Majorca to coagulate milk and in tropical America for dish washing. **Medicinal:** Fruit: Laxative and tonic, poultice; pounded into a pulp was used by King Hezekiah to cure a malignant swelling. Used to cure warts, skin ulcers. Leaf decoction: Remedy for diabetes, calcification in liver and kidney.

And they knew that they were naked; and they sewed FIG leaves together.... Genesis 3:7

H: Teenah.   F: Figuier.   G: Feigenbaum.   I: Fico.

CULTIVATION
Zones 8–11. Humus-rich soil, moist, well drained. Sun, with dry summers, as rain can split the ripening fruit. Propagation by seed, cuttings, or aerial layering.

GREEK JUNIPER Juniperus oxycedrus   Cupressaceae
Mediterranean

The *arar* of Jeremiah, often referred to as heath, is believed by most biblical scholars not to refer to a true heath. It is impossible to be exact as to the true identity of evergreens in the Bible, so the juniper is but one candidate for the heath. *J. phoenicea* berries were found in a 3rd Dynasty grave.

A pyramidal evergreen tree to 33 feet high with sharp, pointed leaves. More drought and cold resistant than the cypress. Male cones are ovate; female cones are small with a berrylike structure when ripe.

ANCIENT AND MODERN USES
Wood: Fragrant, close grained, durable. Construction, mummy casings, fencing, railwaysleepers. **Berry:** Culinary, flavoring for meats, gin and liqueurs. Used in embalming. **Cosmetic:** Used in perfume industry for men's fragrances, soap. The fragrance is obnoxious to insects and used as moth repellant. **Medicinal:** Oil: Stimulant, antiseptic. Cade oil was used to treat corneal opacities. Leaf extract: Antibiotic. **Heartwood and Root:** Centuries ago, in dentistry, to treat pain; to kill lice; for snakebite; used on penis as contraceptive; remedy for leprosy, skin diseases. Still used for eczema, psoriasis, and as ingredient in antiseptic soap.

For he shall be like the HEATH in the desert.... Jeremiah 17:6

31

H: Arar. F: Génvérier oxycèdre. G: Wacholder. I: Ginepro.

CULTIVATION
Zones 7–10. Sunny, well-drained soil. Propagation from cuttings in winter or by grafting.

L AURESTINUS Viburnum tinus Caprifoliaceae
Mediterranean

Biblical scholars believe that this plant may be the *tidhar,* also translated "plane," which has otherwise not been identified. In Aramaic the word has been translated as *murneyon,* which is akin to the Arabic term for this plant.

Laurestinus grows on the Carmel and in the upper Galilee. It is an evergreen to 10 feet. The flowers are white or pinkish, followed by black fruit.

The glory of Lebanon shall come to you, the cypress, the PLANE and the pine.... Isaiah 60:13

H: Moran, Tidhar. F: Laurier tin. G: Lorbeerschlinge. I: Lauro salvatico.

CULTIVATION
Zones 7–10. Well-drained soil, sun, or light shade. Propagation from cuttings in summer or seed in fall.

M ULBERRY Morus nigra Moraceae
West Asia

This tree, native to Persia, has been cultivated in Palestine since 200 C.E. Its name, *morus,* is derived from the Latin, *mora*—delay. It is the last tree to sprout in spring.

Medium sized to 30 feet, with a short, rugged trunk branching crookedly to form a broad, irregularly dome-shaped crown. The dark-green, heart-shaped leaves are toothed and lobed. Mulberries are deciduous or monoecious, and sometime a tree will change sex. The fruit is green at first, then pink, and finally purple. Its red juice was used to provoke elephants to fight.

ANCIENT AND MODERN USES
Wood: Dark and very hard. Furniture. **Bark:** Tannin. **Leaf:** Food for silkworms. (*M. alba* used after 1434). **Fruit:** Fresh or dried, made into jams and wine. Used to fatten sheep to make them more digestible. Dye in medieval times. **Medicinal:** Bark: Laxative, vermifuge. Unripe fruit: May cause hallucinations, nervous stimulation, and upset stomach.

They might provoke the elephants to fight, they showed them the blood of grapes and MULBERRIES. I Maccabees 6:34

H: Tut. F: Mûrier noir. G: Schwarze maulbeere. I: Gelso nero.

CULTIVATION
Zones 6–10. Grows under wide range of conditions. Best in fertile well-drained soil, sun. Propagation by cuttings in winter.

MYRTLE Myrtus communis Myrtaceae
Mediterranean

Myrtle grows on hillsides in Israel and is one of the plants used for the feast of *Sukkot*. Myrtle is symbolic of justice and divine generosity. The Hebrew name is a popular name for women. The plant was held sacred by the ancient Greeks.

An aromatic evergreen shrub to 6–8 feet with shiny, elliptical leaves. The white flower is followed by an ovoid blue-black berry.

ANCIENT AND MODERN USES
Wood: Hard and well grained. Walking sticks, furniture, tool handles. **Bark and Root:** Tanning for the finest Turkish and Russian leather. **Leaf:** Spice, pillow stuffing, bridal wreaths for virgins, tea. **Berry:** Food flavoring, a winelike drink. **Cosmetic:** Breath sweetener. Ground Leaf: Baby powder. Leaf: Perfume sachets and toilet water *(eau de Cologne)*. **Medicinal:** Oil from leaf—bladder and lung diseases.

I will plant in the wilderness, the cedar...and the MYRTLE, and the oil tree.... Isaiah 41:19

H: Haddas. F: Myrtle. G: Myrte. I: Mirto.

CULTIVATION
Zones 8–11. Moist, well-drained soil in sun or light shade. Propagation by cuttings or from seed.

OAK, TABOR OAK Quercus Ithaburensis Fagaceae
Mediterranean

Among the oak species in ancient Israel, the Tabor Oak is one of the mightiest in the oak forests including *Q. Aegilops, Q. Ilex, Q. Calliprinos*. Today, only remnants of these forests have survived, either in groves or as single specimens. Many oaks in biblical times were associated with worship, burial sites, ritual and religious customs.

The Hebrew for oak, *alon,* is associated with the Hebrew word for "god," *El*.

The Tabor oak is deciduous and can attain 400–500 years and can regenerate from its stump. Leaves are ovate to oblong, hairy and soft with serrated margins. A long time may lapse between pollination and fruit maturation. The size of the fruit, the acorn, varies.

ANCIENT AND MODERN USES
Wood: Strong, heavy, close-grained, hard, durable elastic. Building, furniture, fuel. **Fruit:** Acorns eaten in Mediterranean countries, especially in times of famine. Can be ground, roasted and made into bread "Bread of Hunger," fodder. **Symbolism:** Power, longevity, pride, splendor, unity, strength.

They sacrifice on the tops of the mountains, and make offerings upon the hills, under OAK, poplar, terebinth, because their shade is good. Hosea 4:13

H: Alon.   F: Chêne.   G: Eiche.   I: Quercia.

35

CULTIVATION
Zones 7–10. Deep, well drained soil. Possess extensive root systems and dislike transplanting. Propagation by fresh seeds or cuttings.

OLEANDER Nerium oleander Apocynaceae
Mediterranean

Some scholars agree that oleander is a candidate for the "rose" of the Bible. It grows along stony riverbanks in Israel.

This shrub, with a milky juice, can reach 12 feet. The leathery leaves are narrow and glossy. The clusters of white, pink, salmon, or red flowers appear at the top of the branches. All parts of the plant are poisonous.

ANCIENT AND MODERN USES
Medicinal: Leaf: Preparation of cardiac glucoside. Externally used against lice. In India it figured in cases of suicide. Very poisonous!

I was exalted like a palm tree in Engedi, and as a ROSE plant in Jericho.... Ecclesiasticus 24:14

H: Harduf. F: Oléandre. G: Lorbeerrose. I: Nerio comune.

CULTIVATION
Zones 8–11. Well-drained soil, full sun. If it gets leggy it can be severely pruned in spring. Propagation from seed in spring or from cuttings in summer.

OLIVE   Olea Europeae   Oleaceae
Mediterranean

Cultivated over 6,000 years ago, mainly for the oil extracted from crushing its fruit. Olive trees are mentioned in the story of Noah and over 150 times in the Bible. The common olive is one of the seven species with which Israel was blessed. Oil is symbolic of goodness and purity, and the tree is a symbol of peace and happiness. Olives were a symbol of fertility: "Thy children [shall be] like olive plants round about thy table." (Ps. 128:3). It is the emblem of the State of Israel. The importance of the olive was demonstrated when Moses exempted men from the military if they worked in its cultivation. Many references to gardens in Scripture seem to refer to olive groves.

Arabs have a saying. "Take oil internally, externally and eternally to enjoy a long healthy life." This slow-growing evergreen tree can grow to 30 feet and for 1,000 years or more. It is difficult to kill, for when the tree is cut down new sprouts appear from the roots around the old trunk. Olives can even bear when the trunk is hollow. The willowlike opposite leaves, with a grayish-green upper side and a whitish and hairy lower side, are followed by fragrant, white flowers.

The fruit is green when unripe, becoming purple-black, and has a bitter taste. Olives are cultivated for seven years before fruiting and reach maturity after 15–20 years. A full-sized tree produces half a ton of fruit annually. Olive oil is the only edible oil made from a fruit instead of a nut or seed (i.e., corn, peanut, safflower). It produces fruit longer than any other fruit tree.

Olive trees in the Garden of Gethsemane. 19th century engraving by W.H. Bartlett.

ANCIENT AND MODERN USES

Wood: One of the heaviest and toughest. Richly grained and very difficult to work. Construction, ornaments, household utensils, tool handles, statues. **Twigs and Leaves:** Often included in garlands. **Fruit Pulp:** Oil: Used for anointing, sacrifices, cooking, lighting, ingredient for ink, leather softener. Used to ripen sycamore

Pouring oil over a mummy.

figs, greasing fingers of wool weavers. **Leaf:** Wreaths, writing material; in ancient Syracuse, names of banished individuals were recorded on olive leaves, from which the term "petalism" is derived. **Pits:** Used in mills as fuel and fertilizer manufacture of molded products and plastics. **Cosmetic:** Fruit: Soap, deodorant combined with spices. Tonic for hair and skin. Flowers steeped in oil for perfume. **Medicinal:** Bark: Vulnerary *(Gomme d'Olivier).* Leaf: Astringent, antiseptic, febrifugal.

Anointing.

Healing gums and boils. Demulcent, laxative, combined with alcohol as hair tonic, skin lubricant. Antidote for poison, vermifuge. Used in the 4th century B.C.E. for contraception by combining with oil of cedar, lead, or frankincense and smearing the vagina. Greece and Crete, where it is widely ingested, have the lowest incidence of cardiovascular illness in the world, and recent studies found that the oil reduces cholesterol levels.

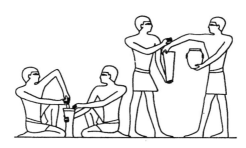

Mixing aromatic oils in containers. Old Kingdom.

And, lo, in her mouth was an OLIVE leaf freshly plucked....
Genesis 8:11

Beam olive press.

H: Zayit. F: Olivier. G: Ölbaum. I: Olivo.

CULTIVATION
Zones 8–11. Poor soil. Winters should be sufficiently cool to induce flowering with hot and long summers. Needs ample moisture when fruits are forming. Propagation by seed in fall or from stem cuttings in winter, from suckers, or by grafting.

PISTACHIO Pistacia vera Anacardiaceae
Mediterranean

Several species of pistachio are found in Israel, including *P. terebinth.* They are referred to in the Bible in different contexts. Their place of origin is uncertain. *P. vera* is a close relative of *P. atlantica* and is frequently grafted onto its stump.

The *botneh* mentioned in the Bible and the Talmud, recurring in local places, is evidently the cultivated pistachio.

A deciduous tree to 30 feet. Leaves are compound of 3–5 oval leaflets. Flowers precede leaves and are red. Nuts, produced after four years, are about 1 inch long and grow in clusters like grapes. They are protected from dust by a

thin, ivory-colored shell. Under favorable conditions the shell splits along the sutures before harvest. After 20 years the tree produces 40–50 pounds of nuts annually. Trees may live for centuries.

ANCIENT AND MODERN USES
Wood: Furnishings, agricultural implements. **Nut:** Food, confectionery, ice cream, sausages, oil (low in saturated fat). **Galls on Leaf:** *P. terebinth:* Tanning, employed in India to dye silk. **Resin:** Embalming, chewing gum, adhesive. In ancient days, to preserve wine.

Carry down the man a present,...spices and myrrh, NUTS, and almonds.... Genesis 43:11

H: Elah. F: Pistachier. G: Pistazienbaum. I: Pistacchio.

CULTIVATION
Zones 8–10. Well-drained soil in full sun with long, hot, dry summers. Propagation from seed sown in fall and winter, or by budding or grafting. Needs male and female trees to produce fruit.

POMEGRANATE Punica granatum Punicaceae
Mediterranean, Persia

The pomegranate has been cultivated in Egypt and Palestine from time immemorial. It is mentioned over 44 times in the Old Testament. Its Hebrew name, *rimmon,* serves as a proper name for places and people. It was among the fruits brought back by the spies Moses sent out and was mentioned by the Israelites in the desert as one of the fruits they had left behind in Egypt.

Pomegranates found in tomb. Egyptian Museum. Turin.

A deciduous shrub or small tree, with glossy oblong leaves. Flowers are orange-red. The fruit is red, hard, thick-skinned, and crowned with a persistent calyx. It contains many seeds surrounded by edible pulp.

ANCIENT AND MODERN USES
Wood: Walking sticks and woodcraft. **Flower:** Red dye. **Fruit:** The calyx serves as a pattern for the crowns of kings and the *Torah,* called *rimmonim;* as a symbol it was often used on coins and served as a motif for sculpture for the capitals in King Solomon's temple. The hems of the high priest's robes were embroidered with pomegranate designs. May even have served for the design of the first musical bells. Mingled with wine. Used in conserves and syrups (*Grenadine*). **Bark and Rind of Fruit:** Red dye for tanning leather (including Moroccan and Cordovan). **Leaves:** Steeped in vinegar used as ink. **Seed:** Symbol of fertility throughout the East. Often used in conserves and syrups.

Collar. Pomegranate flowers. 1350–1300 B.C.E.

Medicinal: Seed: Remedy for tapeworm. Rind: Astringent, for skin problems, gargle for throat irritation, remedy for diarrhea and as vaginal douche. Large doses of rind can cause cramps and vomiting.

Pomegranate shaped perfume bottles 14th -13th cent. B.C.E.

Thy temples are like a POMEGRANATE split open behind thy veil. Song of Songs 4:3

H: Rimmon.   F: Grenadier.   G: Granatbaum.   I: Granato.

CULTIVATION
Zones 9–11. Well-drained soil, sun. Propagation by cuttings or seed.

Basket of pomegranates. Mosaic floor of ancient synagogue. Maon. 6th cent. C.E. (Dept. of Antiquities, Jerusalem).

QUINCE Cydonia oblonga Rosaceae
Asia

First cultivated in Mesopotamia, then in Greece. Some scholars believe that the "apples" of the Bible were quinces.

Slow-growing tree up to 20 feet, with oval leaves wooly underneath, and pink, orange, or white flowers. Tree begins to bear in the second year but bears profitably in 10 years. The skin of the pear-shaped, pleasantly aromatic, acidic fruit is covered with fuzz.

ANCIENT AND MODERN USES
Fruit: Hard and sour made palatable on cooking. Marmalade, jam. **Medicinal:** Fruit: Ingredient of skin lotions. Vermifuge. Seed: demulcent, expectorant, and tonic known since ancient times.

But of the TREE of knowledge of good and evil, thou shalt not eat of it.... Genesis 2:17

H: Chabush.   F: Cognassier.   G: Quitte.   I: Cotogno.

CULTIVATION
Zones 6–9. Moist, deep soil; sun. Propagation by seed obtained from overripe fruit and grafting.

RUSSIAN OLIVE Elaeagnus angustifolia Elaeagnaceae
West Asia

Growing at the mouths of dry streambeds, also along the coasts of Syria and Lebanon.

Deciduous tree to 20 feet, has small leaves, grayish-green above and silvery and scaly beneath. Small, usually bisexual greenish-yellow flowers, appear in clusters in the leaf axis. The fruit is ovoid and tasteless or, in cultivated form, almost as large as an olive and edible. Although still sometimes called "wild olive," it has no botanical relation to the true olive.

ANCIENT AND MODERN USES
Wood: Hard and fine-grained. Carved images, fuel. **Bark and Leaf:** Tanning, fodder. **Fruit:** Arabs dry and pound them to produce a kind of bread called "Trebizond dates." Russians produce a strong wine–as strong as vodka. **Oil of Fruit:** Not used for food because the fruit is rather inferior.

I will plant in the wilderness the cedar, the acacia tree, and the myrtle, and the OIL tree. Isaiah 41:19

H: Ez Ha'Shemen. F: Eléagne. G: Oleaster. I. Eleagno.

CULTIVATION
Zones 7–9. Most soils. Propagation by seed or cuttings.

SYCAMORE FIG   Ficus sycomorus   Moraceae
Mediterranean

This was one of the most important fruit trees in ancient Egypt, especially appreciated for its shade; it may live to 1,000 years. It grows in the coastal plain and Jordan valley, Jericho, and Canaan. The prophet Amos was a "dresser of sycamores."

An evergreen to 30–40 feet and sometimes attaining a trunk girth of 20 feet. It has a huge, spreading crown, an enormous root system. The outer bark peels in small papery flakes. The heart-shaped leaves are slightly rough, with entire margins (unlike *F. carica*). Unlike most fig species the fruit is borne in clusters on fruiting branchlets on the trunk and main branches. Yellow-red when ripe,

the fruit is up to 2 inches across. Amos knew the importance of pricking each fruit at the right stage in its development to make it edible. It is pollinated much like the true fig. The fruit is inferior to that of the common fig, but like it, can produce several crops annually.

ANCIENT AND MODERN USES
Wood: Strong, soft, light, porous, fine-grained, and very durable. Egyptian coffins, construction, furniture, boxes, doors, temple statuary, household articles, fuel. **Fruit:** Food. Most of the fig remnants found in Egyptian tombs were *Ficus sycamorus,* not *F. carica.* **Medicinal:** Fruit: Vermifuge and laxative. Juice of rind: Remedy for snakebite, ear pain. Leaf: Snake and scorpion bites.

Sycamore fig tree. Note the gashed fruit. Thebes.

46

Sycamore Fig goddess. Grave of Sennedjam 19th century B.C.E.

I was an herdsman, and a gatherer of SYCAMORE FRUIT....
Amos 7:14

H: Shikma.   F: Sycomore.   G: Sykomoren feige.   I: Sicomoro.

CULTIVATION
Zones 10–12. Full sun to part shade. Propagation by cuttings
or aerial layering.

TAMARISK   Tamarix aphylla   Tamaricaceae
Mediterranean

Some biblical scholars believe that the tamarisk was the
source of *manna* in the desert. Bodenheimer of the Hebrew
University described *manna* as a sweet secretion of various
insects. The word *manna* may be derived from the Egyptian
word *mennu*—food—or *ma hu*—Hebrew for "what is it?" The
Arabs called it *mann al samma*—heavenly bread. Some
modern scholars identify the *manna* as derived from lichen or
allied species of plants found in Arabia and Yemen.

This giant tamarisk grows in sandy areas. A deciduous tree up to more than 40 feet high with small, feathery leaves that excrete salt through special glands in its leaves. Roots rapidly penetrate the soil, and once they reach groundwater a tree can grow without irrigation. The pink flowers are followed by minute seeds.

ANCIENT AND MODERN USES
Wood: Hard, heavy. Ploughs, water-wheels, walking sticks, bed frames, bowls for milking Bedouin camels, charcoal. **Bark:** Tanning. **Leaf:** Fodder. **Galls:** Mordant in dyeing and tanning.

Now Saul was sitting in Gibeah, under the TAMARISK tree in Ramah, with his spear in his hand.... I Samuel 22:6

H: Eschel.   F: Tamaris.   G: Tamariske.   I: Tamarisco.

CULTIVATION
Zones 8–11. Sandy soil with good drainage. Can tolerate very dry conditions. Propagation from hardwood cuttings in winter, semi-ripe cuttings in late spring.

TRAGACANTH   Astragalus gummifer   Leguminoseae
Asia Minor, Syria, Iran

Biblical scholars believe that the "gum" mentioned in the Old Testament refers to tragacanth, which grew on Mount Hermon.

A perennial shrub to 2 feet high with pinnate leaves. The large taproot, smooth branches and downy twigs bear stiff, yellow spines to 2 inches long. The woody parts and the taproot excretes a gummy substance, *Gum Tragacanth*, when injured. From vertical knife incisions, the gum emerges in ribbonlike strips, which have to be collected in the absence of rain.

ANCIENT AND MODERN USES

Gum: Calico printing, confectionary, salad dressings, as a stabilizer in ice cream. Furniture, automobile and leather polish. **Cosmetic:** Toothpaste and hand lotion. **Medicinal:** Suspending medium for insoluble powders, adhesive in pills. Emulsifier in insect repellant.

A little balm and a little honey, GUM, myrrh, pistachio nuts, and almonds. Genesis 43:11

H: Keder.   F: Tragacanthe.   G: Astragel.   I: Astragalo.

CULTIVATION
Zone 7–9. Not cultivated as a crop. The gum is collected from wild plants.

VINE, GRAPE Vitis vinifera Vitaceae
Mediterranean

The grapevine was the first cultivated plant mentioned in the Bible. It appears over 300 times—in every book except Jonah and Ruth, from the 9th chapter of Genesis to the 14th chapter of Revelation. The art of wine making is attributed to Noah. A rich vocabulary is associated with the vine in the Bible. Grapes were cultivated in all lands bordering the Mediterranean. Many place names in Palestine, such as Mount Carmel (hill of the vineyard), are linked to the vine. The most famous biblical vineyard was that of Naboth. Ahab coveted its site for an herb garden. We hear of drunkenness in stories of Noah and Lot, but alcohol was forbidden to the priests during their ministry.

A fast-growing climbing shrub with long tendrils. The lobed leaves are deciduous. The minute greenish clustered flowers are followed by berries.

Grape harvest and wine production, 18th Dynasty.

Expressing juice from grapes and pressing the juice into a tied bag with pressure from poles. Beni Hassan.

Over-indulging at a
party.

Guests carried away
after a banquet.
Beni Hassan.

ANCIENT AND MODERN USES
Berry: Food. Dried—raisins. Juice made into wine or vinegar; the word *vinegar* is a combination of *vin* (wine) and *aigre* (sour). Wine is preferred to water in warm countries because it causes a loss of body warmth, the opposite of water. Champagne, ingredient for cognac, brandy, vermouth, liqueur. Ink, dye. **Seed:** Contains 15% oil—soap and linseed substitute. **Leaf:** Food. **Waste Products:** Fodder, tannin, cream of tartar. **Medicinal:** Antiseptic, ancient anaesthetic, and used to reduce pain in capital punishment. **Symbolism:** Peace and tranquility. Emblem of Israel. Jesus compared himself to a "true vine" of which his apostles were the branches.

For the Lord thy God bringeth thee into a good land...a land of wheat, barley, and VINES. Deuteronomy 8:7–8

H: Gefen.   F: Vigne.   G: Weinstock.   I. Vite.

CULTIVATION
Zones 6–10. Humus-rich, well-drained soil, sun or part shade. Needs cool winters and low humidity. Propagation by cuttings in winter.

51

WALNUT   Juglans regia   Juglandaceae
West Asia

Only one biblical reference may refer to the walnut. From pre-historic times the walnut spread to many countries. In eastern Jerusalem there is a place called "Valley of Walnuts."

A wide-branched tree to 50 feet high with a spread of 30 feet. Brownish-grey bark. Leaves are aromatic and coppery brown as they unfold and are made up of nine oval leaflets. Flowers before leafing.   Male flowers are pendulous, pale-yellow catkins and turn black. Erect female flowers grow on terminal spikes. The fruit is ovoid, green, and leathery and occurs in groups of one to three. The hull encloses the tan walnut. The tree fruits when 5–8 years old and may produce for 50–100 years.

ANCIENT AND MODERN USES
Wood: Light, tough, and strong. Construction, fine furniture and shipbuilding, Now used for cabinet work, paneling veneer, rifles and guns. The Caryatid Temple on the Acropolis is made of walnut wood. **Bark of Young Branches:** Used by North Africans to massage and lighten teeth. **Leaf:** Tannin. Can be used instead of smoking tobacco. **Sap:** Sugar in Caucasus extracted like maple sugar. **Nuts:** Contain 60% fat—eaten fresh or

pickled in vinegar. **Nut Casings and Leaves:** Dried and pulverized, can be used for pepper. Pounded walnut and oil used in Circassian dish *Charkasia.* **Oil:** Wood polish, lamp-oil, cooking, tannin, artist's paint (especially used by Venetian masters). **Green Husk:** Yellow dye, fodder. **Cosmetic:** Hair tint, soap. **Medicinal:** Oil: Suntan, skin disorders, mouthwash, insect repellant, antitumor compound (*Juglone*), laxative. Leaf: Astringent, tincture used in pulling teeth and decoction for mouthwash.

I went down into the garden of NUTS.... Song of Songs 6:11

H: Egoz.   F: Noyer.   G: Walnuss.   I: Noce.

CULTIVATION
Zones 4–10. Deep, rich soil and sun. Fallen leaves said to be toxic to other plants. Propagation with fresh seeds or by grafting in late winter before new buds appear.

WILLOW   Salix alba   Salicaceae
North Africa and Europe

Scholars dispute whether the biblical plant is this willow or the Euphrates poplar. Both trees grow along streams. Willow boughs are among the four species included in the *lulav* for the Feast of Sukkot.

A deciduous, low-growing tree, usually lacking a central trunk. It is often used to control erosion. The oblong hairy leaves and flowers are arranged in catkins, males and females on separate trees. The minute greenish flowers are followed by many-seeded fruit.

ANCIENT AND MODERN USES
Wood: Durable, light, soft, resilient, tough, and easily worked. Ploughs, troughs, shoes, sieves, toothpicks, tool handles, cricket bats. Before the use of plastic and fiberglass was used for artificial limbs. Boats, fuel and manufacture of paper pulp. **Branches:** Fodder. **Charcoal:** Pencils for artists. **Bark:**

Tannin. **Twig:** Plant supports, weaving baskets, twine, paper, chair seats. The Dutch stabilized sea defenses with *polder mats*—huge mattresses bound with willow saplings weighed down with stones. **Gall on Leaf:** Dye for veils. **Leaf:** Substitute for tea. **Seed:** Inferior grade of lamp-wick. **Medicinal:** Bark, leaf, twig and fruit: Salicylic acid, ingredient of aspirin. Medicinal value already known in Egypt 1500 B.C.E. (Synthetic aspirin introduced in 1899). Antirheumatic drug and substitute for quinine.

And ye shall take on the first day boughs of... WILLOWS of the brook.... Leviticus 23:40

H: *Aravah levenah.* F: *Osier blanc.* G: *Silberweide.* I: *Salcio bianco.*

CULTIVATION
Zones 2–10. Frost hardy. Prefers cool, moist soil with sun or part shade. Propagation from seed or cuttings year-round or by layering. Seeds remain viable for short periods. If they fall on wet ground under suitable conditions, they will germinate within 12 hours.

WORMWOOD Artemisia herba—alba Compositae
Mediterranean

Bitterness of wormwood is mentioned several times in Scripture. Wormwood is also used metaphorically to describe calamity as "her end is bitter as wormwood...." (Prov. 5:4) or "who turn judgement to wormwood" (Amos 5:7).

A small shrub, to three feet. Gray, fragrant foliage with insignificant fragrant flowers.

ANCIENT AND MODERN USES

Leaf: Beverage–ingredient of absinthe, vermouth, fodder. Bedouins use dried leaves for tea and to fumigate poultry with the smoke of burning leaves.
Medicinal: Tonic, stimulant, vermifuge. Used externally as antiseptic.

Behold, I will feed them with WORMWOOD, and make them drink the water of gall.... Jeremiah 23:15

H: La'anah.   F: Armoise.   G. Wermut.   I: Artemisia.

CULTIVATION

Zones 4–10. Open, sunny site in well-drained soil. Propagation by cuttings or division.

Table. Thebes.

Headrest. Thebes.

Chair. Thebes.

Harp, guitar, double pipe, lyre, square tamborine. Thebes.

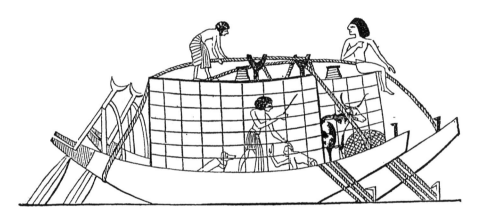

Cattle and goods boat. Thebes.

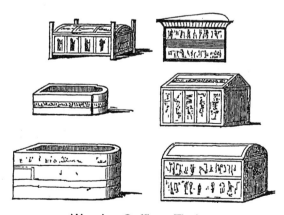

Wooden Coffins. Thebes.

The word incense (Latin *incendere,* to burn) has the same literal meaning as the word perfume, which is the aroma given off with the smoke *(perfumus)* of any odoriferous substance when used.

Incense performed the function of "pleasing the nostrils of the gods" by burning. Many have no natural fragrance but give off sweet-smelling fumes when burnt. The identification of these substances in the ancient Near East is very difficult, so many of the ancient terms remain unidentified.

Incense has played an important role in the services of the Holy Tabernacle and in the ritual services of the Temple. We find specific injunctions concerning the composition and preparation of the holy incense (Exodus 30:34): "Take unto thee sweet spices, stacte and onycha and galbanum; sweet spices with pure frankincense...."

Incense was not only sold as small balls of grains, but reliefs show us discs and cakes or lumps of incense.

Incense was burned as a fragrant perfume by Jewish priests in religious ceremonies (Lev. 16:12) and it was one of the treasures brought to the infant Jesus by the wise men (Matth. 2:11).

ALOE Aloë succotrina Liliaceae
Mediterranean

Aloes are mentioned in both the Old Testament and the New Testament. Most modern commentators consider these passages as referring to two different plants. The Old Testament aloe is likely to have been *Aquilaria agalocha,* Eaglewood (see below).

Aloë succotrina is a succulent plant, named after its native island, Socotra, in the Indian Ocean, south of Arabia. Its thick, sword-shaped leaves form a tight rosette. The red, bell-shaped flowers grow on tall spikes, followed by oval fruit. The aromatic, bitter juice is extracted from the leaves.

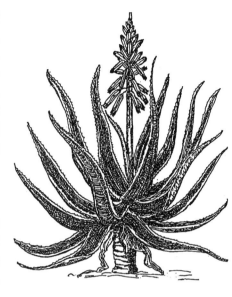

ANCIENT AND MODERN USES
Leaves: Fiber. **Juice of Leaves:** Used in embalming in ancient Egypt. **Medicinal:** Promotes digestion, vermifuge, skin softener.

Nicodemus also, who had at first come to him by night, came bringing a mixture of myrrh and ALOES about a hundred pounds weight. John 19:39

H: *Ahalim.*   F: *Aloès.*   G: *Aloë.*   I: *Aloe.*

CULTIVATION
Zone 9–11. Sun, sand. Can be harvested year-round. Propagation from suckers or pups.

BALM, THORN TREE, FALSE BALM   **Balanites aegyptiaca Zygophyllaceae**
N. Trop. Africa, Arabia

Also called "Jericho balsam;" common in the Jordan valley and Dead Sea region. Some biblical scholars identify it with the

"Balm of Gilead," *Commiphora opobalsamum.* It was used as an ingredient of holy oil.

A desert tree with thorny branches, leathery leaves. The green flowers bloom in winter and are followed by green drupe with a sweet pulp, which ripens in spring. It resembles dates in shape and size and is also known as "Desert Date."

ANCIENT AND MODERN USES

Wood: Compact, fine-grained, hard. Ships, clubs, ploughs, walking-sticks, turnery, axes, wooden bowls. Since it produces little smoke, firewood for burning indoors. **Spiny Branches:** Pens for animals. **Bark:** Fiber. Poison for fishing. **Leaf:** Food, spice. **Fruit:** Oil for cooking, alcoholic beverage in Congo. Source of *Betu Oil,* soap. Fodder. In West Africa and Chad used for breadstuffs and soup. **Cosmetic: Seed**: Body lotion. **Medicinal**: Roots and Bark: Purgative and vermifuge; to speed the healing of wounds and as an antidote for snake bites.

Take of the choice fruits of the land in your vessels, and carry down the man a present, a little BALM, and a little honey,.. Genesis 43:11

H: *Tsori, Zaqum Mizri.* F: *Dattier du desert.* G: *Ägyptischer Zahnbaum.* I: *Dattero deserto.*

CULTIVATION
Zone 9–11. Grows in arid tropical conditions. Propagation by seed.

C ASSIA Cinnamomum cassia Lauraceae
China, Burma

An expensive and exotic import in biblical times, as was cinnamon. Spices and perfumes were confined not only to religious context of holy oils and incense, but their sensual and aphrodisiac qualities were greatly prized.

The bark is coarser and darker than that of *C. Zeylanicum.* The tree has smooth, strongly veined leaves. Flowers are small, white or cream in delicate sprays, and are followed by small, green, fleshy berries containing a single seed.

ANCIENT AND MODERN USES
Leaves, Twigs, and Immature Fruit: Oil used in incense.
Buds: Used instead of cloves to season dishes.

And of CASSIA five hundred, according to the shekel of the sanctuary,... Exodus 30:24

H: Ketziah.   F: Laurier casse.   G: Kassien zimtbaum.   I: Lauro cassia.

CULTIVATION
Zone 9–11. Tropical and subtropical conditions with high rainfall.

C INNAMON Cinnamomum zeylanicum Lauraceae
Sri Lanka

Trade in spices has existed since earliest times with lands on the Indian coast and the Mediterranean along ancient trade routes. The cinnamon tree is mentioned three times in the Bible. Cinnamon was an ingredient in the holy oil that was used in the Tabernacle to annoint officiating priests and sacred vessels.

This evergreen tree may reach 40 feet. The papery bark is light brown; the aromatic, oblong green leaves are 5–7 inches long. The yellow flowers are followed by dark purple berries. Cinnamon is obtained by letting the bark dry into "quills."

ANCIENT AND MODERN USES
Dried Bark: Spice. **Bark, Leaves, Stem, and Roots:** Contain essential oils: ingredient for anointing oil, also used in mummification, food flavoring, including soft drinks, especially of the "cola" type, chewing gum. **Leaf:** Wreath. **Cosmetic:** Perfume. **Medicinal:** Oil: (Eugenol) antiseptic, ingredient for drugs, dentifrices, and disinfectants.

Take thou also unto thee the chief spices...and of sweet CINNAMON half so much.... Exodus 30:23

H: Kinamon. F: Cannellier de Ceylan. G: Zimtbaum. I: Cannella.

CULTIVATION
Zones 11–12. Deep, free-draining soil. Needs tropical conditions with high rainfall, full sun. Propagation by seed sown in fall or by cuttings.

E AGLEWOOD Aquilaria agallocha   Thymelaeceae
E. Africa, N. India

This tree is believed to be the aloe mentioned in the Old Testament in the verse referred to below. It was in great demand for its fragrance and oil. The tree secretes an aromatic resin, especially when it is old.

A tall evergreen tree to 100 feet with a girth of 5 to 8 feet with alternate leaves. Flowers are in clusters followed by the fruit, a two-valved capsule. Under certain conditions, and only in some trees, the wood becomes gorged with a dark resinous aromatic juice and constitutes the drug *agar*. The average yield of a mature tree is 6–8 lb.

ANCIENT AND MODERN USES
Wood: Pale, light, does not float on water. Fragrant–especially partially decayed wood called *agar;* when powdered used to repel fleas and lice. **Oil:** Incense, fumigation. **Fiber:** Rope. **Bark:** Cloth, paper; 30,000 rolls were given to a Chinese emperor in 284 C.E. **Cosmetic:** Oil: Perfume. **Medicinal:** Carminative, diuretic, stimulant, tonic.

Your robes are all fragrant with myrrh and ALOES and cassia. Psalms 45:8

H: Ahaloth. F: Agalloche. G: Agallochabaum, I: Calambucco.

CULTIVATION
Zone 9–11. Sandy or clay soil. High humidity and rainfall.

Spices were used as an ingredient of aromatic body ointments.

Perfuming an embalmed body.

FRANKINCENSE Boswellia sacra Burseraceae
Iran, Iraq, Somalia

It is mentioned 22 times in the Bible. Numbered among the Temple treasures and traded throughout the ancient world; its incense was imported into Israel by the Phoenicians via the famous spice route. There are numerous species of *Boswellia,* which also supply incense. The word *Frankincense* is derived from Old French *franc encens* "free lighting."

A small, scrubby tree with tiny, pinnate leaves and small greenish or whitish flowers. The tree often grows out of boulders where monsoon rains have blown seeds into cracks. The resin is harvested by making gashes in the gray, papery bark. A milky-white fluid

oozes out to dress the tree's wounds, and after a week the resin—shiny, yellowish, or reddish—appears, aromatic and bitter. One tree yields about 10 pounds of resin annually.

ANCIENT AND MODERN USES

Gum: Incense, also used today in ceremonies of the Roman Catholic Church. **Cosmetic:** Ingredient of perfume. **Medicinal:** Antiseptic, antifungal, and anti-inflammatory. The resin contains flavonoids that cause the bronchi of lungs to dilate, so relieves lung infections and asthma. Breath freshener. Disinfectant for burial purposes.

Harvesting frankincense in the Middle Ages. Paris 1675.

Take sweet spices, stacte...sweet spices with pure FRANKIN-CENSE.... Exodus 30:34

H: Levonah. F: Oliban. G: Echter weihrauchbaum. I: Olibano.

CULTIVATION

Zones 10–12. Sun, limestone soil, and monsoon rains. Propagation by cuttings.

G ALBANUM   Ferula galbaniflua   Umbelliferae
Persia

Like cassia and cinnamon and other ingredients of holy oils and incenses, it was imported into Israel. It is mentioned twice in the Old Testament.

Finely cut, greyish, pinnate leaves and large, flat umbels of greenish-white or yellow flowers are borne on 5 foot high stout stems. The fruit is thin and flat.

The gum is obtained from incisions to the stem and rootstock. The milky juice solidifies and turns yellow on exposure to light and air. It forms a bitter aromatic gum, composed of irregular masses of tears, orange-brown to bluish-green and brownish-black. Galbanum comes on the market in lumps that consist of these tears.

ANCIENT AND MODERN USES
Gum: Varnish. A constituent of incense. **Food:** Frequent flavor components in nonalcoholic beverages, candies, baked goods. Oil, meats and gravies. **Cosmetic:** Gum: Perfume, soaps **Medicinal:** Gum: Carminative, stimulating expectorant with other remedies.

And the Lord said unto Moses: Take unto thee sweet spices, stacte and onycha, and GALBANUM....Exodus 30:34

H: Helbenah.   F: Galbanum.   G: Galbanpflanze.   I: Galbano.

CULTIVATION
Zone 9–11. Perennial. Sun, well-drained soil. Propagation by seed.

L ADANUM Cistus ladaniferus Cistacae
Mediterranean

Gum–myrrh, a resinous substance, is believed to be obtained also from some other species of Cistus. It is widespread in Gilead.

An evergreen shrub with oval green leaves coated with a shiny resin that, in the heat of the day, becomes semi–liquid and fragrant. The white flowers are followed by small capsuled fruits. The soft, dark-brown or black, gummy exudation is collected by drawing through the plant a bunch of leathery thongs, to which the gum sticks, or by combing out goats' beards, to which the gum adheres. The gum is then sold in golden, spiral pieces.

ANCIENT AND MODERN USES
Stem, Leaf: Incense; still used in Eastern churches. **Cosmetic:** Used in perfumes. **Medicinal:** Salve, deodorant, asthma and dysentery. Stimulant and expectorant.

Some balm and some honey, gum, ladanum.... Genesis 43:11

H: Lot. F: Ciste landifère. G: Spanische zistrose. I: Cisto ladinifero.

CULTIVATION:
Zones 8–10. Warm, sunny location with rather dry soil. Propagation from cuttings or seed.

MYRRH   Commiphora abyssinica   Burseraceae
Somalia, Nubia, Arabia

It is difficulty to determine the ancient source of myrrh used for incense. There are 160 species of *Commiphora* alone and of these, two are in Arabia, one on the island of Socotra, and 41 in northeast Africa.

Shrub or small tree with thorny branches. A gum-resin is obtained from wounds in the stem. The resin is dried on the stem; then the red-brown clumps are harvested.

ANCIENT AND MODERN USES
Cosmetic: Perfumes primarily fashionable in the Oriental world.
Medicinal: Embalming, wounds, treatment of eye diseases and body odors, stimulant, stomachic, astringent.

Workers filling containers with myrrh extracted from the tree. Deir el-Bahri, Egypt 15th century B.C.E.

Your robes are all fragrant with MYRRH and aloes and cassia. Psalms 45:8

Then, opening their treasures, they offered him gifts, gold and frankincense and MYRRH. Matthew 2:11

H: Mir.   G: Commiphore.   G: Myrrhenbaum.   I: Commifora.

CULTIVATION
Zone 9–11. Propagation by seed or cutting.

SPIKENARD   Nardostachys jatamansi Valerianaceae
India, Himalayas

Spikenard was imported from India in ancient times. It (nard) is mentioned three times in the Old Testament and twice in the New Testament as an aromatic plant valued for its rhizomes.

A perennial herb. Leaves and aerial stems are short and hairy. It flowers in small clusters. All parts of the plant contain an essential aromatic oil.

ANCIENT AND MODERN USES
Cosmetic: Whole plant: Perfume and hair-dyeing. **Medicinal:** Oil: Treatment of nervous disorders.

While the king was on his couch, my NARD gave forth its fragrance. Song of Solomon 1:12

H: Nard.   G: Nard indient.   G: Indische narde.   I: Spignardi.

CULTIVATION
Perennial. Tropical. Not available now.

S TORAX Styrax officinalis Styracaceae
Mediterranean

The resin *stacte,* an ingredient of the holy anointing oil, was believed to be a product of *S. officinalis.* The plant seems to have changed as it no longer produces this resin. Some scholars identified the biblical plant with balm.

A many-branched, small, deciduous tree to 20 feet, with heart-shaped leaves. When young, silvery-white on the underside. Small, fragrant, white, bell-shaped flowers bloom in June, followed by a round drupe–hairy, fleshy, bitter, and with a toxic pulp.

ANCIENT AND MODERN USES
Trunk and Branch: Resin or balm (only from very old trees). **Seed:** Oil: perfume. **Medicinal:** Treatment for coughs, ointment for swellings.

Ishmaelites came from Gilead with...BALM.... Genesis 37:25

H: Libneh refui. F: Storax. G: Storaxbaum. I: Storace.

CULTIVATION
Zones 8–11. Moist, well-drained soil in sun or light shade. Propagation by cuttings in summer.

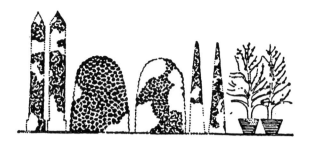

Heaps and cones of incense. 1300 B.C.E.

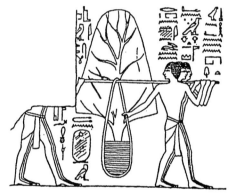

Incense trees imported from Punt.1350 B.C.E.

Myrrh trees from Punt, after a relief in Queen Hatshapsut's temple. 15th century B.C.E.

Vegetables, compared to grains and fruit seeds, perish easily and so have rarely been discovered in archeological excavations. This is equally true of melons and tubers, known from illustrations only. It has been difficult, therefore, to deal with them historically and to know when they were introduced. Only in Egypt with its arid climate, have some remains of vegetables been found. As pollen and other studies progress, scientists will be able to begin to trace the development of vegetables and tubers in the ancient Near East.

Vegetables added nutrition and variety to the daily diet of rich and poor alike. Chick-peas were cultivated in Mesopotamia 8,500 years ago and found in ancient Jericho. Garlic was considered a necessity for the laborers who constructed the pyramids. Cucumbers and leeks were part of the dietary memory of ancient Israelites.

ARUGULA, ROCKET   Eruca sativa   Cruciferae
Mediterranean

Most scientists agree that this is the garden vegetable mentioned in the Bible as *orot* (II Kings 4:39). Found in the Upper Galilee, Jordan Valley, and Dead Sea areas. Bedouins collect it as a pot herb. The ancients called it the "vesper flower," because of its night fragrance.

Low growing to 24 inches. Lower leaves divided into lobes. Flowers are creamy-yellow or white.

ANCIENT AND MODERN USES
Seed: Substitute for pepper, source of *Jamba* oil. **Leaf:** Salad green, spice. **Cosmetic:** Leaf: Deodorant. **Medicinal:** Was used to treat eye infections, digestive and kidney problems. A decoction was used to protect against the effect of dog bites. It was used as an aphrodisiac throughout ancient times.

One of them went out to gather HERBS.... II Kings 4:39

H: Gargir.   F: Roquette.   G: Gartenrauke.   I: Ruca.

CULTIVATION
Zones: 7–10. Annual. Ready for harvesting after 40 days. Young leaves have better flavor. Propagation from seed.

BEAN   Vicia faba   Leguminosae
Mediterranean

The bean is mentioned twice in the Bible and is the first vegetable harvested in spring. It was one of the earliest domesticated crop plants.

An erect annual to 5 feet. The hollow stem is branched mainly in the upper part. The ovoid leaves are divided into 2–6 pairs. The small, white, sweet-pea-like flowers, marked with a purple spot, are followed by large green pods.

ANCIENT AND MODERN USES
Bean: Mixed with wheat for flour, eaten fresh, boiled, dried, or roasted, a meat extender,

skim-milk substitute. Made into cakes called *tamiya* in Egypt, fodder. **Stem:** Camel fodder.

In ancient Egypt priests were forbidden to eat beans because they were considered unclean. In ancient Greece magistrates were elected by casting beans.

Take thou unto thee wheat and barley, and BEANS.... Ezekiel 4:9

H: Sheut.   F: Fève.   G: Saubohne.   I: Fava.

CULTIVATION
Zones 6–10. Annual. Young plants need staking and should not be overwatered. Harvested in 2–3 months after planting. Propagated from seed.

BLACK CUMIN   **Nigella sativa**   **Ranunculaceae**
Mediterranean

After much confusion about identity, the "fitches" of Isaiah are now generally agreed to be *Nigella sativa,* the so-called "nutmeg flower" (no relation to the nutmeg).

Fennel-like leaves and white or blue buttercup-like flowers. The fruit is a five-celled pod with many black, pungent seeds.

ANCIENT AND MODERN USES
Seed: Ingredient for bread—Russian rye bread, cakes, and curries. It is said that Egyptian women ate seeds to achieve a full figure, considered a sign of beauty in Egypt. **Medicinal:** Vermifuge, jaundice. An Arab proverb states that "in the black seed there

is medicine for every disease, except death." Ethiopians pounded leaves for skin disorders.

When he hath made plain the face thereof, doth he not cast abroad the FITCHES...? Isaiah 28:25

H: Ketza.   F: Nigelle.   G: Echter schwarzkummel.   I: Nigella.

CULTIVATION
Zones 7–10. Annual to 24 inches. Full sun, fertile, well-drained soil. Propagated by seed. Seedlings hate being transplanted.

BLACK MUSTARD   Brassica nigra   Cruciferae
Mediterranean

Growing around the Sea of Galilee and farther north. Often found as weed among cereals. Considered by most translators to be the seed described in the parable of Jesus as "the smallest of all seeds." (Not true, as orchid seeds are smaller). In Jesus' day, the smallest quantity of something proverbially small is compared with this seed.

An annual to 6 feet high or more. Large leaves at the base of the plant, with a strong central stem. Yellow flowers are followed by 1-inch-long pods containing brown seeds.

ANCIENT AND MODERN USES
Young Leaves: Food. **Seeds:** Contain 30% oil, ingredient of table mustard. **Cosmetic:** Lubricant for soft soaps. **Medicinal:** Seed oil. Ingredient of mustard plasters. Oil increases flow of saliva and gastric juice; used as an emetic to cure poisoning.

And he said, "With what can we compare the kingdom of God, or what parable shall we use for it? It is like a grain of MUSTARD SEED, which, when sown upon the ground, is the smallest of all the seeds on earth. Mark 4:30

H: Hardal.   F: Moutarde noire.   G: Senfkohl.   I: Mostarda.

CULTIVATION
Zone 7–10. Annual. Lime-rich soil, weed free, not too wet. Crop rotation should be practiced. Propagation from seed.

CHICK-PEA   Cicer arietinum   Leguminosae
Mediterranean, West Asia

Chick-peas were found in prehistoric sites in Jericho. The word *hamitz* is similar to the Arabic *humus.* Scholars believe that the Hebrew term for provender alludes to this plant.

A 2-foot annual with small leaves and white or reddish flowers followed by a two-seeded pod.

ANCIENT AND MODERN USES
Pea: Food—fresh or dried, flour. Boiled or roasted provides maximum nourishment for a minimum of expenditure (yields up to 1000 lb an acre). Substitute for coffee. Still a popular food of the poor, especially in India, Africa, and South America. Humus and felafel, popular Middle Eastern dishes, are made from the peas. **Whole plant:** Fodder.

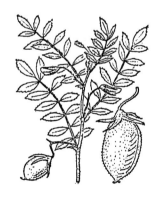

And the oxen and the asses that till the ground will eat salted PROVENDER.... Isaiah 30:24

H: Himtza. F: Pois Chiche. G: Kichererbse. I: Cece.

CULTIVATION
Zones 7–10. Annual. Propagated from seed after frost. Light, loamy soil.

CHICORY Cichorium intybus   Compositae
Mediterranean

Chicory is one candidate for the bitter herbs of Passover.

A perennial to 3 feet with tough stems and long, lobed, basal leaves. The bright-blue flowers close at noon. After ripening, the heads close and conceal the fruit. Rain forces the heads to open and disperse the seeds.

ANCIENT AND MODERN USES
Leaf: Food, fodder, blue dye. **Root:** Coffee substitute, seasoning. **Medicinal:** Leaf: Sedative, laxative. Seed: Demulcent oil. Dried root: Diuretic, tonic.

And they shall eat the flesh...with BITTER HERBS. Exodus 12:8

H: Olesh tarbuti. F: Berbe de capucin. G: Zichorie. I: Cicoria.

CULTIVATION
Zones 4–10. Annual or perennial. If grown as leaf vegetable, plant in fertile, humus-rich, well-drained soil. Propagated from seed or by root division.

C ORIANDER Coriandrum sativum Umbelliferae
Asia Minor

Coriander was known to the Israelites during their captivity in Egypt. In their desert wanderings they described *manna* as the size of coriander seeds.

Parsley like aromatic leaves with umbels of tiny white flowers followed by small, round, aromatic seeds.

ANCIENT AND MODERN USES
Seed: Flavoring food and beverages, including gin and vermouth, tobacco products. **Cosmetic:** Seed: Perfumes, soaps. **Medicinal:** Seed: Stimulant, carminative. If eaten in excess, a narcotic. In Mexico used to enhance flavor of coffee.

And the house of Israel called the name thereof manna; it was like CORIANDER seed.... Exodus 16:31

H: Gad Hasadeh.   F: Coriandre.   G: Koriander.   F: Coriandro.

CULTIVATION
Zones: 7–12. Annual to 1–3 feet. Propagation by seed.

C UMIN Cuminum cyminum Umbelliferae
Mediterranean

Cumin seed, found in an Egyptian grave of the 18th Dynasty, is a powerful aromatic spice, similar to caraway seed but larger, with a disagreeable taste.

Leaves are divided into a few threadlike segments. Small, white flowers are followed by the small, oblong, aromatic seed.

ANCIENT AND MODERN USES
Seed: Spice: Mixed with flour in bread, curry, and kebabs, Leiden cheese, liqueurs. **Cosmetic:** Seed Oil: Used in perfume. **Medicinal:** Oil: Disinfectant, digestive disorders; crushed seeds relieve dizziness. Cumin was used by the ancient Israelites as a healing remedy following circumcision.

Doth he not cast abroad the fitches, and scatter the CUMIN...?
Isaiah 28:25

...For ye pay tithe of mint and anise and CUMIN....Matthew 23:23

H: Kamon. F: Cumin. G: Echter römerkümmel. I: Cumino.

CULTIVATION
Zones 9–12. Annual to 12 inches. Frost tender. Light, well-drained soil in a sunny position. Propagation by seed.

DANDELION Taraxacum officinale Compositae
Temperate Zones

One of the candidates for the "bitter herbs" of the Passover Seder.

A common perennial with toothed oblong leaves. The yellow flowers open in the sun.

ANCIENT AND MODERN USES
Seed: Bird feed. **Leaf:** Food, fodder, **Dried Leaf and Flower:** Diet drink and herb beer, wine. **Flower:** Yellow dye. **Root:** Magenta dye, roasted and ground made into coffee that has tonic and stimulant properties but no caffeine. In WW II the Russian dandelion was a source of rubber, extracted from the latex of its roots. **Medicinal:** Root: Gallstones, jaundice, and other liver problems. Dandelion extracts are used in antismoking compounds.

And they shall eat the flesh in that night...roast with fire...and with BITTER HERBS. Exodus 12:8

H: Shein Ha'aryeh. F: Dent de lion. G: Löwenzahn. I: Dente di leone.

CULTIVATION
Zones 3–10. Perennial. A pesky weed.

D ILL   Anethum graveolens   Umbelliferae
Mediterranean, temperate Asia

Mentioned only once in the New Testament.

An annual to 3 feet high with a hollow stem, ferny leaves, and umbels of yellow flowers. It is common in the Holy Land, both in its wild and cultivated forms. It may often be found in abandoned fields and along the roadside It has been widely grown since ancient times for its pungent seeds, which contain aromatic oils.

ANCIENT AND MODERN USES
Leaves: Salads, soups, sauces.
Seeds: Food: Dill vinegar seasoning pickles, chewing gum, roasted seeds, substitute for coffee. **Cosmetic:** Soap, perfume. **Medicinal:** Ripe seeds are used as a carminative.

Woe to you, scribes and Pharisees, hypocites! For you tithe mint and DILL and cummin and have neglected the weightier matters of the law.... Matthew 23:23

H: Sheveth.   F: Fenouil puant.   G: Dill.   I: Aneto odoroso.

CULTIVATION
Zone 5–10. Tolerates moist soil. Harvested in 6 weeks from the time of sowing. Propagation by seed.

ENDIVE   Cichorium endivia   Compositae
Mediterranean

Close relative to chicory. A candidate for the "bitter herbs" used for the Passover Seder.

It produces a dense rosette of leaves.   Flower stems to 3 feet with blue flowers.

ANCIENT AND MODERN USES
Leaf: Culinary. **Seed:** Used in sherbets.

Watering plants by means of a *shaduf.*

And they shall eat the flesh in that night, roast with fire...and with BITTER HERBS. Exodus 12:8

H: Olesh.   F: Endive.   G: Endivie.   I: Indivia.

CULTIVATION
Zones 4–10. Annual or biennial. Mostly frost hardy. Full sun in fertile, moist, well-drained soil. Propagation by seed.

GARLIC   Allium sativum   Liliaceae
Mediterranean

Grown in Egypt and the Near East since earliest times. Was part of the diet of pyramid workers, who consumed 1.5 million pounds of it. When a drought hit the country, creating a shortage, pyramid workers refused to work, launching the first recorded labor strike. The *Codex Ebers,* an Egyptian medical record (1550 B.C.E.) lists 22 garlic prescriptions.

The common garlic is much like an onion above ground, but the bulb is compound, its tight papery sheath enclosing several daughter bulbs or "cloves," wrapped together in a pinkish-white, papery skin. Flowers are tiny and pink.

ANCIENT AND MODERN USES
Bulb: Food: Fresh, dried, or powdered. **Medicinal:** Juice used for intestinal infections, lowering blood pressure, preventing blood clots, also used to counteract arteriosclerosis, respiratory ailments, snake bites. Ancient Israelites used the cloves for treatment of melancholy and hypochondria. National Cancer Institute files report lower incidence of cancer in countries like France and Bulgaria, where a great deal of garlic is eaten. In Russia it was used to fight flu epidemics, and since WW II it has become known as the "Russian penicillin." Used in Europe to disinfect burial grounds to prevent the plague from spreading and has become an alternative to insecticides such as DDT. Guardian Spray®. A garlic solution, is a good pesticide for backyards and house plants. Use of aged garlic extract, a deodorized supplement, avoids garlic breath, as does eating parsley. Modern users claim it is able to reverse dandruff. Mixed in dog food, it is said to discourage fleas.

We remember the fish... and the GARLIC. Numbers 11:5

GOURD, WILD Citrullus colocynthis Cucurbitaceae
N. Africa, W. Asia

This is the wild gourd of the desert. An attractive fruit that almost poisoned Elisha's men.

The wild gourd resembles the cucumber. A prostrate plant, the stems radiating from a tuberous perennial rootstock. The deeply lobed leaves are under 4 inches long. The 3-inch fruit is striped, yellow and green. The very bitter fruit yields a drastic purgative which, when taken in excess, may prove fatal.

ANCIENT AND MODERN USES
Fruit Pulp: When dried as powder, Arabs use for kindling, repels moths from wool. **Seed:** Food in Central Sahara. **Seed Oil:** Illuminant. **Medicinal:** Fruit: When dried to a powder used as a purgative.

One of them went out into the field to gather herbs, and found a wild vine and gathered from it his lap full of wild GOURDS, and came and cut them up into the pot of pottage, not knowing what they were. But while they were eating of the pottage, they cried out, "O man of God, there is death in the pot!" II Kings 4:39–40

H: Paqquoth. F: Coloquinte. G: Bitterzitrulle. I: Coloquinda.

CULTIVATION
Zone 8-11. Grown much the same way as a pumpkin. Well-manured soil with good drainage and a long growing season. Propagated by seed.

Cooking and baking. Thebes.

L EEK Allium porrum Liliaceae
Central Asia

It is questionable whether the leeks, referred to by the biblical Hebrew word *hatzir*, are the true leeks or whether the word refers to fenugreek *(Trigonella foenum—graecum)*. Both were known in the Holy Land.

Leeks were one of the foods the Israelites craved in the desert. *Hatzir* literally means "herbs." Leeks have always been the food of the poor in the Orient and were regarded as the food of humility. Leeks, unlike onions, do not have a bulbous base. The leaves are broad and concave, and their sheathing bases form a tight cylinder for the edible part. The white flower appears in the second year in a ball-like cluster.

ANCIENT AND MODERN USES
Leaf: Food. Same properties as garlic, but to a lesser degree. **Medicinal:** Leaf: When crushed can be used to ease the sting of insect bites, disinfectant.

We remember the fish... and the LEEKS.... Numbers 11:5

H: Shum Hakarash. F: Poireau. G: Porree. I: Porro.

84

CULTIVATION
Zones 5–10. Biennial. Sunny, well-drained soil. Propagation from seed or bulbs.

L ENTIL   Lens esculenta   Leguminosae
Mediterranean

Mentioned five times in the Old Testament. Ancient containers with lentil markings were found in Sumeria, and a lentil puree was discovered in 12th-Dynasty tombs in Egypt. Lentils were Jacob's meal in the biblical tale of Genesis, so important in the patriarchal saga. They have often been referred to as "poor man's meat," since lentils are easy to grow and full of proteins. Lentils were bartered by the Egyptians for cedar wood from Lebanon, as recorded in the story of the "Voyage of Wenamum." They were shipped in enormous quantities.

To 18 inches high. Leaves are pinnate, the upper ones modified into tendrils. The small blue flowers are followed by short, flattened pods, each containing one or two green, greenish-brown, or reddish seeds.

ANCIENT AND MODERN USES
Husks, Dried Leaf, Stem: Fodder. **Seed:** Food, flour for bread, fodder, source of commercial starch for textiles and printing industries. Romans crated an obelisk taken from Egypt, which now stands in front of St. Peter's in Rome, with 2,880,000 lb of lentils, a precursor of our packaging "peanuts." **Medicinal:** Seed: Remedy for constipation. Poultice for ulcers.

And he sold his birthright unto Jacob. And Jacob gave Esau bread and pottage of LENTILS.... Genesis 25:33–34

H: Adhashah. F: Lentille. G: Linse. I: Lenticchia.

CULTIVATION
Zones 8–11. Annual. Light, sandy, well-drained soil in full sun. Marginally frost hardy and a cool season crop. Propagation by seed.

L ETTUCE Lactuca sativa Compositae
Mediterranean

A candidate for "bitter herbs." Grown for its succulent, crispy leaves. It is a plant picked before it is fully grown. When allowed to mature, lettuce develops a tall stem with alternate leaves and panicled heads of yellow flowers.

Gardeners in a vegetable garden. Beni Hassan.

ANCIENT AND MODERN USES
Leaf: Food: Fresh or cooked. **Medicinal:** When allowed to go to seed, it contains latex that has a narcotic effect and is used as an opium substitute. In ancient Egypt, lettuce was a symbol of fertility and used for impotence.

And they shall eat the flesh in that night, roast with fire...and with BITTER HERBS. Exodus 12:8

H: Hasah.   F: Laitue cultivée.   G: Kopfsalat.   I: Lattuga.

CULTIVATION
Zones 7–12. Annual. Well-drained soil in full sun or part shade. Propagation by seed.

MARJORAM, OREGANO   Majorana syriacum, Origanum syriacum Labiatae
Mediterranean

Modern scholars have identified the "hyssop" of the Bible with this plant. It is found in dry places, growing among rocks. A bunch of hyssop was used for sprinkling blood on the door lintels and posts at Passover. Its hairy leaves can absorb liquids. It is unrelated to the *hyssop officinales* of Europe.

A strong, multi stemmed shrub with ovate, hairy, gray leaves. The small, white flowers are grouped in spikes. The fruit is a small nutlet.

ANCIENT AND MODERN USES
Leaf: Tea and spice. **Medicinal:** Tonic, antiseptic, carminative, digestive aid. Used for purification of lepers.

And ye shall take a bunch of HYSSOP and dip it in the blood that is in the basin.... Exodus 12:22

H: Ezov. F: Origan. G: Dost. I: Origano.

CULTIVATION
Zones 8–9. Annual. Sun and well-drained soil. Propagation by seed or by root division.

MINT, HORSE MINT Mentha longifolia Labiatae
Asia, Africa, Europe

Out of 23 different species of mint, three species, including horse mint, are found in Israel along ditches, swamps, river-banks, and even seasonally moist places. It is generally considered a weed. The fragrant mint of the New Testament was probably horse mint.

A 3-foot tall, strong scented pe-rennial herb with stout stems and 2-inch-long notched, grayish-green, spear-shaped leaves covered with tiny hairs. Flowers are lilac.

ANCIENT AND MODERN USES
Fresh leaves: Food: Seasoning in Indian chutneys. Essential oils used for flavoring. Scattered over floors of synagogues. Herb pillows. **Dried Leaves and Flowering Tops:** Substitute for peppermint oil in flavoring candy. **Medicinal:** Disguises disagreeable taste, aids digestion.

Woe to you, scribes and Pharisees, hypocrites! For you tithe MINT and dill and cummin and have neglected the weightier matters of the law... Matthew 23:23

H: Mitba'a. F: Menthe sauvage. G: Wilde minze I: Menta.

CULTIVATION
Zone 4–9. Most are frost hardy. Sun, need moisture. Invasive, spreading by runners. Propagation from seed or by root division.

MUSKMELON   Cucumis melo   Cucurbitaceae
East Africa

It is generally believed that the Hebrew name denotes the garden CUCUMBER *(C. sativus),* but since it is native to South Asia, this is unlikely. More probably, the biblical verse refers to *C. melo,* which is a wild species from East Africa and includes forms with long, narrow fruits resembling the garden cucumber. This melon is also known as cantaloupe—a name dating to the 18th century.

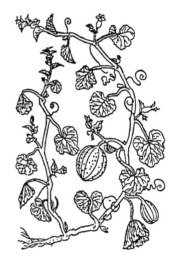

A trailer with hairy, kidney-shaped leaves. The flowers are yellow. The yellow or green fruit varies in size and shape as well as sweetness.

ANCIENT AND MODERN USES
Fruit: Food—raw or cooked. **Leaf:** Eaten raw or steamed. **Seed:** Edible, oil. The Lebanese believe it repels bedbugs. **Medicinal:** Antivinous, demulcent, diuretic, emetic.

We remember the fish... in Egypt...the CUCUMBERS and the melons.... Numbers 11:5

H: Kishu.   F: Melon Commun.   G: Melone.   I: Melone.

CULTIVATION
Zones 8–11. Annual; needs a long, hot summer to produce sweet fruit. Can be trained over plastic for heat to circulate. Propagation by seed.

ONION Allium cepa Liliaceae
Mediterranean

There are more than 500 species of onions, some edible, some ornamental.

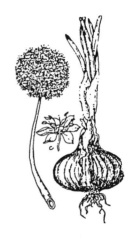

A. cepa is called the Egyptian onion. Onions have been known to man for over 4,000 years and are represented in many Egyptian tomb paintings. Onions were found in the breasts of mummies, onion peel on their ears and eyes. Onions were considered a necessity for workers building pyramids. Nine tons of gold were reportedly paid for onions and garlic to sustain the laborers. Only mentioned once in the Bible. In Yiddish "to grow like an onion" is an insult, but it is certainly a compliment to "know one's onion!"

A perennial herb. This large bulb produces hollow stems terminating in umbels of pink or white flowers.

Egyptians with fruit, flowers, and onions (in a triangular rack), 2590 B.C.E.

Tying up onions for offerings.

90

ANCIENT AND MODERN USES
Bulb: Food: Fresh, boiled, fried or roasted, dehydrated; also made into onion salt or powder. **Skin:** Dye. **Medicinal:** Laxative, antiseptic and vermicidal, antibiotic. Reduces hypertension, high blood sugar (diabetes), and cholesterol. The ancient Egyptians swore by onions —some were accused of worshiping them as a god, so Egyptian priests were forbidden to eat them.

We remember the fish, which we were wont to eat in Egypt...and the leeks and the ONIONS.... Numbers 11:5

H: Bezel.   F: Oignon.   G: Zwiebel.   I: Cipolla.

CULTIVATION
Zones 4–11. Prefer a sunny, open position in well-drained soil. Propagation from seed or bulbuls.

REICHARDIA   Reichardia tingitana   Compositae
Mediterranean

This is another candidate for *bitter herb* possibly eaten at the Passover Seder.

The poppy-leaved *Reichardia* is a desert plant. The flowers are yellow with a dark purple base.

ANCIENT AND MODERN USES
Leaf: Culinary.

They shall eat the flesh that night... with unleavened bread and BITTER HERBS. Exodus 12:8

91

H: Tamrid Marokani. F: Roquette. G: Gartenrauke. I: Ruca.

CULTIVATION
Zones: 7–10. Annual. Propagated by seed.

SAGE   Salvia judaica   Labiatae
Mediterranean

Some scholars have considered this plant, or the almond, the model for the seven-branched candelabrum, a traditional Jewish symbol. The branched inflorescence of the sage plant when pressed reminds us of this candelabrum.

The paired leaves are wrinkled. Violet flowers are tubular, two lipped, with the lower lip flat but the upper lip boat shaped.

ANCIENT AND MODERN USES
Leaf: Spice, flavor wine. **Medicinal:** When drunk as tea, reduces perspiration, nervous conditions; antiseptic, gargle for laryngitis. Extended use can cause poisoning.

And he made the CANDLESTICK of pure gold:.. even its base, and its shaft; its cups, its knobs, and its flowers, were of one piece with it. Exodus 37:17

H: Marva. F: Sauge. G: Salbei. I: Salvia.

CULTIVATION
Zones 8–10. Perennial to 3 feet. Full sun and light-textured soil. Propagation by seed, cuttings, or division.

WATERMELON   Citrullus vulgaris   Cucurbitaceae
Tropical Africa

Watermelons have been grown in Near Eastern countries since time immemorial. They are 90% water, so they are invaluable in the desert. The opened fruit was used for plant propagation.

This tropical trailer with hairy, deeply lobed leaves produces a yellow flower about 1 inch across. The fruit is often ellipsoidal, 10 inches or more in diameter, with white, yellow, or red flesh.

ANCIENT AND MODERN USES
Fruit: Food. Rind of fruit preserved in sugar and vinegar.
Seed: Eaten raw, roasted. Used in soups and stews, or ground for bread. **Oil of Seed:** In Africa, extracted and used for soap or lighting. **Medicinal:** Antiseptic and laxative, vermicide. Crude seed extract lowers blood pressure.
We remember the fish, which we were wont to eat in Egypt...the cucumbers, and the MELONS.... Numbers 11:5

H: Avatiah.   F: Melon d'eau.   G: Wasser melone.   I: Melone d'acqua.

CULTIVATION
Zones 8–11. Well-manured soil with good drainage and a long, warm growing season. Propagation by seed.

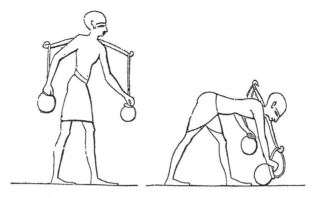

Men watering a garden. Beni Hassan.

Watering through a shaduf,

Vineyard with a watering tank,

Plants that could be used for fabrics and clothing were discovered rather early. Plant fibers augmented those derived from animals and were especially useful in lands without large herds of sheep and goats. The long fibers produced by plants could be twisted into flexible thread and then woven to produce comfortable garments and many other useful items. The basic textile plants remained the same through history until the introduction of synthetic fibers in the twentieth century.

COTTON Gossypium herbaceum Malvaceae
Arabia, Asia

The only biblical reference to cotton is in the story of Esther, which mentions white cotton curtains in the palace at Susa. Cultivated very early in the Indus Valley and Mesopotamia.

Cotton is an annual to 8 feet with deeply lobed leaves and yellow or pink flowers. Its fruit is a capsule surrounded by 3–4 heart-shaped bracts containing several seeds densely covered with long, white, fluffy hairs.

ANCIENT AND MODERN USES
Seed: Fiber for fabric, lamp wicks, cloth, mummy wrappings, stuffing, ropes, carpets. **Seed oil:** Cooking, soap, oil-cake used as fertilizer and fodder. **Stalk:** Paper, fuel. **Hulls:** Fodder, fertilizer. **Flower:** Source of mild honey. **Flower Petal:** Yellow and brown dye. **Medicinal:** Surgical dressing.Seeds

have been used for intermittent fever and as an abortifacient (especially by slaves in the southern United States). Used in treating sexual lassitude. Gossypol, from the glands of the leaves, is the male contraceptive now being studied in China. Oil also used as a vehicle for injections, emollient, and lubricant.

There were hangings of white, fine COTTON...Esther 1:6

H: Koton, Karpas. F: Cotonnier. G: Baumwolle. I: Cotone.

CULTIVATION
Zones 9–11. Annual or perennial. Moist, well-drained soil; long, hot summers in full sun. Propagation from seed or cutting.

F LAX Linum usitatissimum Linaceae
Temperate and tropical

Linen (fiber of the flax plant), mentioned over 100 times in the Bible, is one of the world's oldest textiles. Extensively grown in Egypt, it provided the name for the Nile—*Pishtan.*

Three distinct grades of linen were referred to in the Bible, from the finest gauze to a rough canvas. Much of the linen that has survived is in its natural neutral-colored state. The coarsest linen (Leviticus 6:3) was the ordinary linen. A better linen, "twined linen," mentioned (Exodus 26:1). Fine linen (Esther 8:15).

Preparing flax for linen and rope manufacture.

Flax grows to 3 feet high and has small narrow leaves and five-petaled blue flowers. The fruit is a capsule containing several oleiferous seeds. When flax is grown for fiber the seeds are sown close together so that stems grow straight, with as few branches as possible. Linen fibers are prepared by "retting" and "scrutching" the stems; the stems are then soaked in water to separate the tough fibers and soft tissue. After combing, the fibers are spun.

ANCIENT AND MODERN USES

Stalk: Fiber, paper, sails, cloth (Israelite priests wore linen garments), curtains, wicks for lamps, mummy wrappings, cartonnage (linen and papyrus) used for mummy masks, thread, rope, carpets, insulation, bedding, fishing lines, bags. **Seed:** Bird food. Linseed oil, a drying oil when cold pressed, used for eating; when hot pressed, used in paints, varnishes, printing ink, waterproofing, soft soap, linoleum, oil cloth, thick lithographic varnish. **Cosmetic:** Oil: Hair care. **Medicinal:** Seed: De-

Linen leg-bandages.

mulcent and emollient, laxative; currently believed to help lower cholesterol. Decoction—remedy for burns.

Spinning, unraveling flax. Beni Hassan.

Artistic flax mummy wrappings.

Festive costume. End of the 18th Dynasty.

She seeketh wool and FLAX.... Proverbs 31:13
And Pharaoh...arrayed him in vestures of fine LINEN....
Genesis 41:42

H: Peshet, Bad.   F: Lin.   G: Lein.   I: Lina.

CULTIVATION
Zones 4–11. Annual to 3 feet tall. Rich, moist soil in full sun.
Propagation by seed.

A method of wrapping the dress.

Color is important in every culture; from Joseph's coat to the desert Tabernacle, it plays a significant role in ancient Israel. Egyptian wall paintings and pottery along with Mesopotamian tiles show us multicolored garments, many dyed with plant material. Tombs as well as temples and palaces were lavishly and colorfully decorated. Egyptian hieroglyphics used different colors to express specific ideas.

The language of color has enabled us to express our feelings more adequately. The symbolism of color, however, is different in each society.

When Moses led the Israelites out of Egypt, they carried dyes for later use with them: "And they made upon the skirt of the robe pomegranates of blue, purple, scarlet, and twisted linen." (Exodus 39.24)

HENNA   Lawsonia inermis   Lythraceae
Mediterranean, Arabia, India

Henna is mentioned only in the Song of Songs. It was discovered in Tutankhamen's tomb (3200 B.C.E.). Henna dye is considered to have religious, utilitarian, mystical, and seductive powers. The dye is obtained by soaking leaves in water.

A shrub to 8 feet. The leaves are elliptical, grayish green. Flowers are white and fragrant. Fruit is a capsule.

ANCIENT AND MODERN USES

Wood: Tool handles, tent pegs. **Leaf:** Henna powder to dye hair, palms of hands, soles of feet, nails, leather, mummy wrappings, horse tails, fabrics. In Arabia and Egypt, the night before the wedding is called "night of henna," because the bride's hands and feet are decorated with elaborate henna designs. **Root:** Dye: Dried and ground into powder. **Cosmetic:** Flower: Oil *(Mehndi oil)* long used in Indian perfumery. **Medicinal:** Leaves contain an antibiotic *(lawsone)* astringent, stimulant. Was used as an abortifacient.

Skin designed with henna retains the design for three weeks.

Lady rouging herself. Ramesside Papyrus.

My beloved is to me a cluster of HENNA blossoms. Song of Songs 1:14

H: Yachunun. F: Henné. G: Hennastrauch. I: Alcanna.

CULTIVATION
Zones 10–12. Well-drained sandy soil and full sun. Propagation from seed or cuttings.

M ADDER   Rubia tinctorum   Rubiaceae
Asia Minor

This plant is mentioned only as a proper name in the Bible.

A perennial, creeping herb to 4 feet. The leaves grow in 4–6 whorls. Flowers are greenish yellow. Red berries turn black. The root, about the thickness of a quill, is collected in the third year, freed of its outer covering, and dried.

ANCIENT AND MODERN USES
Root: Red dye *(Alizarin)* used for unguents which are painted on terra cotta statuettes. **Leaf:** Animal fodder. **Medicinal:** Root: Astringent.

After Abimelech there arose to deliver Israel Tola, the son of PUAH.... Judges 10:1

H: Puah.   F: Garance.   G: Farberrote.   I: Robbia dei tintori.

CULTIVATION
Zones 6–11. Well-drained soil, full sun to partial shade. Propagation from seed or by division.

S AFFLOWER   Carthamus tinctorius   Compositae
Mediterranean

Also known as Bastard saffron and False saffron. It is possible that this plant may also be involved in the "saffron" of the Bible. It has been used since 2,000 B.C.E. in Egypt for dyeing mummy grave cloths.

Plant to 4 feet high, with spiny, oblong leaves running down the stem. The orange-yellow flowers with leafy bracts are followed by oblong seeds that contain oil.

Servants bringing necklaces of flowers. Thebes.

ANCIENT AND MODERN USES
Flower: Garlands, also for mummies. Produce a source of red and yellow dye, *carthamin.* Used in ancient Egypt and today in preparation of grease paints. **Young Shoots:** Food. **Seed:** Oil. Cooking; paints, varnish, linoleum. Also a source of *Roghan* or *Alfridi wax.* Food for poultry. Fried seed used in chutney. **Pressed Seed Cake:** Cattle fodder.

Spikenard and SAFFRON, calamus and cinnamon.... Song of Songs 4:14

102

H: Karkom, Kurtas.   F: Carthame.   G. Bastardsafran.   I: Croco bastardo.

CULTIVATION
Zones 7–11. Well-drained soil in full sun. Propagation by seed.

SAFFRON Crocus sativus Iridaceae
Mediterranean

Saffron was mentioned in Egyptian papyrus dated as early as 2,000 B.C.E. A yellow dye is obtained from the stigmas of this crocus. Saffron is the world's most expensive spice, requiring the stigmas of 4,300 flowers for 1 ounce of spice.

A bulbous plant that blooms in fall. The grassy leaves appear at the same time as the stemless lilac or purple flower.

ANCIENT AND MODERN USES
Stigma: Dye, flavoring, incense, embalming. Saffron water was sprinkled on theater benches by the Greeks. **Cosmetic:** Perfume, nail polish. **Political:** Many Jews in the Middle Ages were spice merchants, called "saffron merchants."

The yellow color of the spice was used to mock Jews. They were forced to wear yellow hats for easy identification. In the 20th century Hitler ordered Jews to wear the yellow star to distinguish them from the rest of the population. **Medicinal:** Tinctures, gastric and intestinal remedies, carminative.

Thy shoots are a park of pomegranates, with...spikenard and SAFFRON, calamus and cinnamon.... Song of Songs 4:13–14

H: Karkom.   F: Safran.   G: Safran.   I: Zafferano.

CULTIVATION
Zones 6–9. Sun to part shade. Propagation by division. When grown from seed plants will not flower for 3 years.

Weaving and using a spindle before dyeing. Beni Hassan.

Mixing dyes or ink. Beni Hassan.

The floral world of ancient Israel and the surrounding lands was rich but mainly in springtime. The long, hot, dry summers withered almost everything, leaving only a few autumn blooms. Biblical poetry used the imagery of flowers, and as the Bible was not concerned with horticulture, other flowers were not mentioned.

There were no gardens as we know them, although Egyptian and Mesopotamian royalty occasionally planted exotics at temples, tombs and palaces. Flowers were not used in the religious rites of ancient Israel.The chief use of flowers was for decoration and to provide a pleasant aroma.

The Hebrew terms *perah, tzitz,* and *nitzah* were used for all flowers; *nitzah* was most used to describe the spring flowers.

The flowers of the field consist of a number of plants (Isaiah 40:6). The following are commonly identified among them:

GRAPE HYACINTH Muscari Liliaceae
SQUILL Scilla Liliaceae
TULIP Tulipa montana Liliaceae
DAFFODIL Narcissus tazetta Amarylidaceae
CROWN ANEMONE Anemone coronaria Ranunculaceae
POPPY Papaver rhoeas Papaveraceae
CHAMOMILE Anthemis nobilis Compositae
CROWN DAISY Chrysanthemum coronarium Compositae
RANUNCULUS Ranunculus asiaticus Ranunculaceae
CROCUS Crocus sp. Iridaceae
CYCLAMEN Cyclamen sp. Primulaceae

All flesh is grass, and all its beauty is like the FLOWER OF THE FIELD....The grass withers, the flower fades; but the word of our God will stand for ever. Isaiah 40:6–8

My beloved is gone down to his garden, to beds of spices...and to gather lilies. Song of Solomon 6:2

And the desert shall rejoice, and blossom as the ROSE. Isaiah 35:1

Mummy decorated with flowers.

COLCHICUM, AUTUMN CROCUS Colchicum autumnale Liliaceae
North Africa, Central Europe

Mentioned in the Ebers Papyrus of 1550 B.C.E. as a drug plant, a reference that may have referred to the rose.

This poisonous cormus plant produces dark-green leaves in the spring, followed by purple flowers in the fall. The fruit is a capsule with polished, whitish seeds.

ANCIENT AND MODERN USES
Medicinal: Corms. Seed: Sedative, cathartic, antirheumatic, and gout treatment, psoriasis, certain forms of leprosy. It rivals opium for the honor of being the

oldest plant remedy still in use. Since 1937 employed in plant breeding to double chromosomes and develop new strains of plants.

I am the ROSE of Sharon.... Song of Songs 2:1

H: Shoshanah, Sitvanit. F: Colchique dautomne. G: Herbstzeitlose. I: Efemero.

CULTIVATION
Zones 5–9. Perennial to 1 foot high. Good drainage in sun or part shade. Propagation by small bulbs, actually corms.

GLOBE THISTLE Echinops viscosus Compositae
Mediterranean

One of the candidates for thistles. It grows among shrubs and is common in Samaria and other parts of Israel.

To 4 feet high with stout, spiny stems and gray-green leaves. Flowers are globular, spiny, blue.

ANCIENT AND MODERN USES
Food: Source of *Cangado Mastiche* used for chewing gum.

Cursed is the ground because of you;... thorns and THISTLES it shall bring forth to you. Genesis 3:17–18

H: Kipodan, Dardar. F: Échinope. G: Kugeldistel. I: Echinopo.

CULTIVATION
Zones 3–10. Perennial. Well-drained soil in sun. Propagation through division or seed.

IVY   Hedera helix   Araliaceae
Europe, North Africa

Ivy is found in Samaria and Upper Galilee.

An evergreen vine with woody stems. The leaves, with a rounded base and three to five ovate-triangular lobes, grow on long stalks. Flowers are yellow-green umbels. The fruit is black, globular.

ANCIENT AND MODERN USES
Hardwood: Engraving. **Young Twigs:** Source of a yellow and brown dye. **Leaves:** Boiled with soda can be used for washing clothes. In ancient days formed poet's crown. **Medicinal:** Leaves: In ancient times bound around the brow to prevent intoxication. For this purpose, once boiled in wine and drunk to prevent intoxication by wine.

And when the feast of Dionysus came, they were compelled to walk in the procession in honor of Dionysus, wearing wreaths of IVY. II Maccabees 6:7

H: Kissos.   F: Lierre.   G: Efeu.   I: Edera.

CULTIVATION
Zones 5–11. Perennial; will grow in shade. Propagation by cuttings or seed.

MALLOW   Malva sylvestris   Malvaceae
Mediterranean

Biblical scholars feel that the mallow or the hollyhock *Althea sp.* would fit the context of the verse quoted below.

A plant to 3 feet high with broad, heart-shaped leaves. The flowers are rose-purple with darker veins.

ANCIENT AND MODERN USES
Leaves: Used as substitute for tea. **Seeds:** Edible. **Medicinal:** Leaves used as expectorant, flowers for gargling and mouthwash.

Or is there any taste in the juice of MALLOWS? Job 6:6

H: Halomut. F: Meule. G: Malve. I: Malva grande.

CULTIVATION
Zones 5–10. Perennial. Sunny, well-drained soil, though not too rich. Propagation by seed; often self-seeding.

MANDRAKE   Mandragora autumnalis   Solanaceae
Mediterranean

Mandrake is found in stony places. Many superstitions came to be associated with it. Jews considered mandrake a charm against evil spirits because the root resembles the human figure. It has been associated with ancient fertility rites. Arabs called it devil's apple because of its supposed power to excite voluptuousness.

Mandrake is a stemless perennial related to the potato. The dark-green, wrinkled, oblong leaves form a rosette from which a flower stalk rises bearing a bluish-violet, bell-shaped flower followed by a yellow, plum-sized berry.

ANCIENT AND MODERN USES
Fruit: Food. **Medicinal:** Root used by Egyptians as a charm to promote fertility. Esteemed by the ancients for its narcotic, emetic, purgative properties. The plant is slightly poisonous.

And Reuben went...and found MANDRAKES in the field, and brought them unto his mother, Leah. Genesis 30:14

H: Dudaim.   F: Mandragore.   G: Alraune.   I: Mandragora.

CULTIVATION
Zones 8–10. Well-drained site in semi-shade. Propagation by seed or cuttings.

NETTLE Urtica dioica Urticaceae
Northern and southern hemispheres

Nettles grow in abandoned places. Because of their sting, they are used widely as metaphors.

The plant produces opposite, toothed leaves and minute green and white unisexual flowers in tassel-like clusters.

ANCIENT AND MODERN USES

Leaf: Young plants cooked as vegetables (contain more protein than any other leafy vegetable known; also vitamins A and C, and iron). Commercial source of chlorophyll. Nettle beer and tea, green dye. **Dried Leaf:** Fodder. **Stem:** Fiber made into textile and paper. Fiber is stronger than flax and less harsh than hemp. **Medicinal:** Leaf: Scurvy and vitamin-deficiency diseases. Dried Powdered Leaf: Stops nosebleed. **Cosmetic**: Seed: Ingredient of hair tonic, anti-dandruff shampoo.

And thorns shall come up in her palaces, NETTLES and thistles.... Isaiah 34:13

H: Sirpad. F: Grande ortie. G: Brennessel. I: Orticone.

CULTIVATION
Zones 5–10. Easily grown in sun or shade in most soils. Propagation from seed or cuttings.

POISON HEMLOCK   Conium maculatum   Umbelliferae
Eurasia

The Hebrew word *rosh* is often translated as *poison,* which may also refer to wormwood. The Greek name *conium* means stimulating dizziness.

The plant is found in waste places. The hollow stems are marked with reddish spots. The leaves are pinnately compound; the leaflets, feathery White flowers appear in umbels. When bruised, the fresh plant has a disagreeable, mousy odor.

ANCIENT AND MODERN USES
Medicinal: Leaf. Seed: Painkiller, anticarcinogenic. The extremely poisonous nature of the plant was known In classical times. It was a standard method for executing criminals; Socrates was believed to have been such a victim.

Their grapes are grapes of POISON.... Deuteronomy 32:32

H: Rosh Akod. F: Cigue. G: Schierling. I: Cicuta.

CULTIVATION
Zones 3–10. Biennial or perennial to 8 feet high. Any soil. Propagation by seed or division.

SEA DAFFODIL Pancratium maritimum Amaryllidaceae
Mediterranean

This white-flowered bulb grows along the seashore. Some scholars consider this plant to be the biblical lily.

The fragrant flowers are followed by linear leaves. Flowers bloom only a single night. Fruit capsules contain many black seeds. The spongy cover enables them to float on sea-water.

My beloved is gone down to his garden...to gather lilies. Song of Songs 6:2

ANCIENT AND MODERN USES
Bulb: Edible. The woolly layer between its outer skin and interior provides fiber used for felt shoes and clothing.

H: Havazeleth hachov.
F: Pancratier maritime.
G: Meermachtblume.
I: Pancrazio marino.

CULTIVATION
Zones 8–11. Perennial. Full sun and perfectly drained soil. Propagation by seed or offsets.

STAR OF BETHLEHEM, DOVE'S DUNG   Ornithogalum umbellatum   Liliaceae
Mediterranean

Some scholars consider the dove's dung sold in the siege of Samaria by the King of Syria to be bulbs of Star of Bethlehem, which grow profusely on the hills of Samaria and whose white flowers look like bird droppings.

Leaves are midgreen with a central white stripe. The loose clusters of white flowers with green striping appear at the top of the erect, 12-inch stem.

ANCIENT AND MODERN USES
Bulb: Poisonous unless roasted or boiled and ground into meal.

113

And there was a great famine in Samaria... until an ass's head sold for fourscore pieces of silver and... a kab of DOVE'S DUNG.... II Kings 6:25

H: Hiryon Netzhalav. F: Ornithogale. G: Vogelmilch. I: Latte duccello.

CULTIVATION
Zones 5–10. Plant can become invasive. Well-drained soil, part shade. Propagated from seed or bulb.

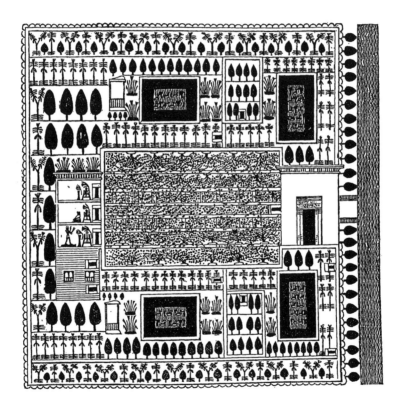

Large, formal garden with a vineyard. Thebes.

G rains and grasses not only played an important role in ancient Near Eastern agriculture, they represented the cultural divide between nomads and peasants. It had not always been so, as the hybridization and intense cultivation of grain crops began among herdsmen who supplemented their diet in this fashion around 12,000 to 8,000 B.C.E.

Grains were the largest component of the daily diet, and all other tasks, including warfare, which stopped during the grain harvest. Good grain storage was a major problem throughout the ancient world.

Ancient Israel, because of its diverse topography and climate, was the only country in the ancient Near East able to grow a large variety of grain crops.

Reeds served as an important material for constructing huts and small boats as well as household and personal items like sandals.

B ARLEY   Hordeum vulgare   Gramineae
Asia

The "corn" of the Bible, is what we in America mostly refer to as "grain." It is mentioned 32 times in the Bible. In ancient times it was thought to be either spring barley, *H. vulgare* or winter barley, *H. hexastichon.* Barley, grown since 5,000 B.C.E. in Egypt, was the cheapest cultivated food obtainable. It can survive heat and drought better than any other cereal and ripens in shorter summers than wheat. Today barley ripens about a month earlier than wheat in Egypt, as it did in 1,290 B.C.E. when a sudden hailstorm destroyed all Pharaoh's barley, which was already mature, but not his wheat. King

Solomon grew great tonnage of barley to feed his 40,000 horses and an unknown number of dromedaries.

Since barley was the food of the poor in biblical times it is used symbolically in the Bible to indicate poverty, destitution and worthlessness. Gideon, a poor and humble man in his dream compares himself to "a cake of barley bread." (Judges 7:13,15).

Seven-row barley ear
Coin. 500 B.C.E.

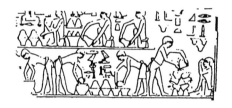

Brewing near a granary. Thebes.

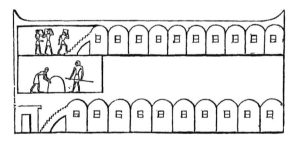

A granary. Beni Hassan.

Barley grows to 2–3 feet. The whiskery ears nod as they mature. The shallow roots develop faster than wheat, and the leaves are wider than those of many other grains. The first sheaves (omer) were offered as a sacrifice on Passover.

ANCIENT AND MODERN USES
Seed: Necklaces found on mummies. Bread when mixed with millet, spelt, or pea meal; yeast for beer (beer is not mentioned in the Bible, but was important in ancient Egypt and Mesopotamia), malt syrup. Used for measurement: 2 seeds = a "finger breadth." 16 seeds = a "hand-breadth". Industrial alcohol used to manufacture artificial rubber and munitions. **Pearled Barley:** Soup. **Stalk:** Fodder, paper. **Medicinal:** Seed: Barley water as demulcent, cooked barley as a poultice. Contains *Hordenine* for bronchitis. Many ancient Egyptian medical uses, including birth prognosis and abortifacient.

And the flax and the BARLEY were smitten.... Exodus 9:31

H: Seorah.   F: Orge commune.   G. Gerste.   I: Orzo commune.

CULTIVATION
Zones 3–11. Well-drained fertile soil and full sun. Propagation by seed.

C OMMON REED   **Phragmites communis   Gramineae**
All continents

This is one of at least five species of riverbank plants mentioned in the Bible.

A bamboolike, creeping cane to 10 feet high; the woody, jointed stems are hollow. The brownish tassels develop in late summer.

ANCIENT AND MODERN USES
Rhizome, Root: Emergency food. **Young Shoots:** Food. **Cane:**

Egyptian containers for lipsticks and eye shadows (mascara). Pens, measuring rods, hedges, mats, flutes, scales, walking canes, sandals, papers, cardboard, cellophane, synthetic fibers, thatch, cement reinforcement, insulation processed into upholstery fillings, fertilizers, fuel. **Seed:** Ground and moistened for candy. **Medicinal:** Rhizome: Diuretic. **Architecture:** Motif for Egyptian columns.

Can the REED-GRASS grow without water? Job 8:11

H: Kaneh. F: Roseau. G: Teichrohr. I: Canna.

CULTIVATION
Zones 5–11. Any soil, as long as it does not dry out in summer. Sun. Propagation from seed or by division.

D ARNEL, TARE   Lolium temulentum   Gramineae
Mediterranean

Darnel is a noxious weed, resembling wheat, that grows only among crops, and damages them because of a poisonous fungus that lives in the grains.

Grass to two-and-a-half feet high. It is smaller than wheat and its ears are more slender.   Each of the chaffy flower groups ends in a short whisker and sheds abundant pollen in late spring. The small seeds germinate freely.

ANCIENT AND MODERN USES
Seed: The poisonous seeds, which contain the mycelium of a fungus, are in some countries some-

times mixed with barley, to give beer an intoxicating effect. **Medicinal:** Plant: Was prescribed for hemorrhage, incontinence. **Seed:** Rheumatism, arthritis, nausea, nosebleeds, intestinal cramps, and trembling limbs.

The kingdom of heaven may be compared to a man who sowed good seed in his field; but while men were sleeping, his enemy came and sowed WEEDS among the wheat, and went away. Matthew 13:24–25.

CULTIVATION
Zone 5–10. Annual. Any soil suitable for cereal. Propagation by seed.

GIANT GRASS Arundo donax Gramineae
Mediterranean

Also known as the "Persian reed," it is common throughout Israel, particularly near the Dead Sea and the Jordan Valley.

A perennial grass to 18 feet with strong, hollow canes. Thin, flat leaves drooping at the tips alternate in two rows up the stems. The plumelike flowers are similar to pampas grass.

Reed coffin. 3100—3000 B.C.E.

119

ANCIENT AND MODERN USES
Cane: Support for vines. Roofing, arrows, fences, basketry, walking sticks, flutes, fishing rods, arrow shafts, kites, clarinets, bagpipes, papers, manufacture of rayons, pens, measuring rods. Egyptian beehives made from reeds held together with mud. Egyptian coffins.

Long flute. Thebes.

Flute players. Thebes.

Now, behold, thou trustest upon the staff of this bruised REED...on which if a man lean, it will go into his hand and pierce it.... II Kings 18:21

H: Avkane shakiah, Kaneh. F: Canne. G: Schilfrohr. I: Canna comune.

CULTIVATION
Zones 9–11. Any soil that does not dry out entirely. Sun to light shade. Propagated by seed or division.

LEMON GRASS Cymbopogon citratus Gramineae
India

Many species of aromatic grasses were imported and were discovered in Egyptian tombs of the 20th and 21st Dynasties. This grass may be the sweet grass of Jeremiah.

The gray-green leaves may reach 6 feet high. The crushed and bruised leaves have a strong lemon fragrance but are tough and inedible. The white bases of the shoots are used for cooking.

120

ANCIENT AND MODERN USES
Leaf Blade, Sheath Husk: Oil, *Oleum citronellae,* flavoring. **Cosmetic:** Perfume.

To what purpose is to Me the frankincense that cometh from Sheba, and the SWEET CANE from a far country? Jeremiah 6:20

H: Sakaneh. F: Herb citron. G: Citrongras. I: Erba di limone.

CULTIVATION
Zones 10–12. Well-drained fertile soil. Needs a long, hot, growing season. Propagation by seed or by division of clumps.

M ILLET Panicum miliaceum Gramineae
India

Millet is mentioned only once in the Bible. It was considered inferior grain and used mainly for fodder.

An annual grass to 2 feet. The leaves are flat and hairy. The flowers and seeds grow in a compound, are branched, and have nodding panicles. The Latin name *miliaceum* was an allusion by Linnaeus to its thousands of seeds, from which we have the word millimeter.

ANCIENT AND MODERN USES
Seed: Food: Porridge, bread. (Contains carbohydrates,10% protein, and 4% fat, so it is very nutritious). Source of *Braga* or *Busa,*

an alcoholic beverage. Bird feed. **Stalk:** Fodder for cattle, but not for horses.

Take thou also unto thee wheat...and MILLET.... Ezekiel 4:9

H: Dochan.   F: Millet.   G: Hirse.   I: Panico miglio.

CULTIVATION
Zones 3–11. Annual. Well-drained soil in sun. Propagation by seed.

SORGHUM, GREAT MILLET Sorghum bicolor Gramineae
East Africa

Great Millet is also called "Jerusalem corn" and may have been the "parched corn" that Boaz gave to Ruth. It has been cultivated since 2,000 B.C.E and is a nonirrigated summer crop in Israel.

The plant grows to 9 feet. The leaves are flat, and the panicles are many branched, producing globular, whitish grain. A single seed head can supply a meal for a large family.

ANCIENT AND MODERN USES
Stem: Fiber, fencing, fuel. **Seed:** Fodder, flour, syrup, alcoholic beverage. Wax of seed coating used in furniture and shoe polish, electric insulation, industrial alcohol. Sorghum starch - adhesive sizing for paper and cloth. **Medicinal:** Diuretic and demulcent as a decoction.

And you, take wheat and barley...and MILLET.... Ezekiel 4:9

H: Durat.   F: Grand millet.   G: Mohrenbartgras.   I: Miglio.

CULTIVATION
Zones 9–12. Soil with humus. Moist. Propagation by seed.

SUGAR CANE   Saccharum officinarum   Gramineae
Tropical Asia

Sugar cane no longer grows wild anywhere in the world, so we are uncertain of its origin. The first historic mention of it was in 500 B.C.E. in China. At first the cane was chewed to obtain sugar. The art of refining sugar may date from the 7th century.

Sugar, a tall grain, requires a tropical climate. The solid, jointed stalks are filled with soft, long fibers. The arching leaves have rough edges. The plumelike tassels contain hundreds of tiny soft lavender-to-dark purple flowers. The canes produce a dark-brown, slightly acid juice, which is extracted and boiled after the leaves have been removed.

ANCIENT AND MODERN USES
Cane: Sugar, molasses. Cooking, candy, rum, industrial alcohol used for explosives, synthetic rubber, used in combustion engines. The residue (Bagasse) used for building material, insulation, for both temperature and sound; manufacture of paper, cardboard, fuel, mulch, plastic material. **Medicinal:** Laxative. **Cosmetic:** Ingredient of hair tonic.

Thou hast bought Me no SWEET CANE with money.... Isaiah 43:24.

H: Kaneh sukar. F: Canne a sucre. G: Zuckerrohr. I: Canna da zucchero.

CULTIVATION
Zones 9–12. Full sun, rich moist soil. Propagation by cuttings.

WHEAT   Triticum aestivum   Gramineae
Mediterranean

Mentioned 175 times in the Bible, but biblical scholars are uncertain just what the wheat was as there are five kinds native to and still wild in Israel today, and at least eight others are cultivated there. *T. aestivum* was the principal cereal grain of Mesopotamia in Jacob's time.

It is a field crop in Palestine since the Bronze Age (3,500–2,000 B.C.E.). Wheat is one of the plants mentioned as "corn" in the Bible and is one of the seven species of the Holy Land. (Wheat and barley are the only grains included in the seven species.) This grain was an important export crop. The first harvest was a temple offering at *Shavuot.* Dates were often reckoned as so many days or weeks before or after the wheat harvest.

An annual grass to 4 feet. Lower leaves are hairy, usually with two ears. The numerous varieties are divided into (1) spring and winter wheat, (2) hard and soft wheat, (3) red and white wheat, (4) bearded and nonbearded varieties.

ANCIENT AND MODERN USES

Stem: Paper, fodder, animal bedding, compost, beehives, packing material, mulch, fertilizer, hats, baskets, chair seats. **Seed:** In biblical times eaten as parched grain and used as a "meal offering." Flour, cereals, starch, paste for glue. Source of alcoholic beverage, beer. Alcohol made into synthetic rubber. **Medicinal:** Starch: Emollient.

Plowing and hoeing. Beni Hassan.

Sowing wheat. Beni Hassan.

A land of WHEAT and barley.... Deuteronomy 8:8

H: Hittah.   F: Blé.   G: Saatweizen.   I: Biada.

CULTIVATION
Zones 5–11. Weed-free soil. Requires a 90-day growing season.
Harvested when stalks are entirely golden and the grains hard.
Propagation by seed.

Harvest scene, cutting, carrying bushels of wheat. Thebes.

Harvest scene, threshing, winnowing, checking the harvest. Thebes.

Kneading and baking bread and cakes. Beni Hassan.

126

Ancient Israel contained large areas of swamps and bogs in which water plants thrived, as they also did in the semitropical Jordan River valley. These plants were cultivated much more widely in the ancient Near East than in modern times.

BULRUSH, CAT-TAIL Typha angustifolia Typhaceae
Northern and southern hemispheres

This may have been one of the water plants of the Bible. Although it grows in many places, huge colonies of it grow along the Nile and along fresh and brackish waters, where they reduce soil salinity. The bulrush is called the "supermarket of the swamps" because it has many uses.

This plant has stout, midgreen stalks crowned by ridged, cylindrical, flowering spikes to 10 feet. Each spike, cigarlike, contains hundreds of minute flowers, male flowers above, female flowers below, without petal or sepal but represented by bristles. The fruit is a small, hairy grain.

ANCIENT AND MODERN USES
Root: Starch (potato substitute), sizing and medium for fermentation, fuel, alcohol; the starch can also be converted to sugars.
Stalk, Leaf: Stalks when peeled taste like cucumbers. Woven articles, chair seats, caulk for canoes, sandals, thatching, paper pulp. Substitute for jute, rope, winnowing-trays, mats. **Flower Cluster:** When papery sheath is

removed, boiled and eaten like corn. **Pollen of the Male Flower:** Flour, food dye. **Seed:** Drying oil for industry, cattle and chicken feed. **Seed Floss:** Insulator, substitute for kapok, stuffing for pillows, mattresses, sleeping bags; vests, spun into fabric, food, tinder (ignites with spark). **Cat-tail Head:** Immersed in kerosene, a torch. **Medicinal:** Seed floss: Dressing burns.

And its canals will become foul...reeds and RUSHES will rot away. Isaiah 19:6

H: Suf.   F: Masse d'eau.   G: Breiter rohrkolben.   I: Tifa.

CULTIVATION
Zones 3–9. Moist soil or shallow water. Propagation from seed or by division in spring.

Bog at the edge of a pond. Amarna.

FLOWERING RUSH **Butomus umbellatus   Butomaceae**
Asia, Europe

Another candidate for *reed grass* mentioned in Genesis 41:2. A botanist traveling in Israel has identified 460 different grasses, so it is impossible to know which of them is mentioned in the different scriptural passages.

Growing to 4 feet tall and 24 inches wide, it has midgreen

leaves, bronze when young, and umbels of pink flowers, partially hidden by the foliage.

ANCIENT AND MODERN USES
Rhizomes: Food by some people in Russia.

And, behold, there came up out of the river seven kine, well-favored and fat-fleshed; and they fed in the REED GRASS. Genesis 41:2

H: Ahu.   F: Butome.   G: Blumen rohr.   I: Butomo.

CULTIVATION
Zones 5–9. Deciduous perennial. Sun, in boggy soil. Propagation from seed or by division in spring.

IRIS, YELLOW FLAG   Iris pseudacorus   Iridaceae
North Africa

Biblical scholars believe this to be one of the plants referred to as "lilies by the rivers." It grows along waterways and marshes.

The beardless water iris is a perennial with large, stout, fibrous roots. The sword-shaped leaves grow to 5 feet. Flower stalks rise to 7 feet and have yellow flowers.

ANCIENT AND MODERN USES
Root: Scent for linen closets, tannin, blue and black dyes. **Powdered Root:** Snuff. **Leaf Fiber:** Paper, nets, canvas cloth. **Flower:** Yellow dye. **Seed:** Substitute for coffee. **Medicinal:** Anti-inflammatory.

I am the rose of Sharon, a LILY of the valleys.... Song of Songs 2:1

H: Irio. F: Iris jaune. G: Wasserschwertlilie. I: Iride gialla.

CULTIVATION
Zones 5–9. Rhizome. Best in shallow water, rich soil, and sunny position. Propagation by division of rhizomes.

LOTUS Nelumbo lotus Nymphaeceae
Egypt

Although the lotus of the ancient Egyptians was a true water lily *(Nymphaea lotus),* the name is now applied to a related plant whose flowers and leaves stand upright above the water. Lotus was sacred to Egypt 5,000 years ago and is represented on Egyptian wall paintings.

Leaves are large, waxy, and nearly circular. Lotuses resemble water lilies but differ in that they raise both their leaves and their flowers well clear of the muddy water. The large, white, fragrant flowers are borne on long stalks that open at night and close around noon the following day. They are followed by flat-topped seed pods.

ANCIENT AND MODERN USES
Rhizome: Food. **Leaf:** Able to shed dirt, because of wax and tiny points, like a bed of nails, now developed as "Lotusan," an ingredient of house paint, roof shingles and auto paint: stays clean for five years without detergent. **Seed:** Ground into flour or roasted. **Architecture:** Flower: Motif for Egyptian columns.

Some historians trace the pattern of the Ionic capital and the Greek fret to the furled petals of the Egyptian lotus bud.

Ramses II with lotus flowers. 19th Dynasty.

And the brim thereof was wrought like the brim of a cup, like the flower of a LILY.... II Chronicles 4:5

H: Lotus, Shoshanah.   F: Lotus.   G: Lotusblume.   I: Loto.

Necklace with lotus blossoms.

CULTIVATION
Zones 10–12. Deciduous perennial rhizome. Heavy loam. Sun, still water, and annual feeding. Goldfish kept in the pool will eat most pests. Propagation by division or seed.

PAPYRUS Cyperus papyrus Cyperaceae
Mediterranean

The word "Bible" is derived from papyrus as is the Greek word for book—*biblos* and the Latin word *biblia.* Both come from the ancient Phoenician port of Byblos. The merchants of Byblos supplied the Greeks with Egyptian papyrus, which they used for paper. Our word paper has its origin in the word *papyrus.*

In ancient Egypt, the papyrus was the symbol of Lower Egypt, whereas the lotus represented Upper Egypt—knotted, as the sign of the union under one scepter.

Papyrus grew in Israel's Lake Huleh and in Egyptian swamps. Although almost extinct in Egypt, it still grows in the Sudan and in Uganda. Moses' cradle, believed to be made of papyrus stems, floated among the papyrus and other waterside plants. Thor Heyerdahl built a large papyrus boat in the 1990s to demonstrate its ocean going possibilities.

Papyrus sandal.

Building a papyrus boat.
Berlin Museum.

Papyrus harvest. Tomb of Uch-hotep Meir. 1950 B.C.E.

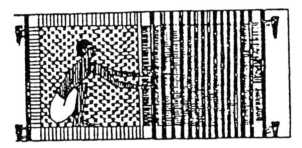

Mat-maker, Tomb of Cheti. Beni Hassan.

Papyrus is a perennial with triangular, smooth stem to l0 feet, composed of pith encircled by a tough rind. Tiny brown flowers bloom on branches.

ANCIENT AND MODERN USES

Stalk: Paper (the Vatican still uses a few sheets for official decrees), boats, sandals, ropes, wrapping paper, cartonnage for mummy casings, bridges, mats, lamp wicks, sieves, chairs pillows, boat caulking, baskets, boxes, sails, cloth, paint brushes (from frayed stalk ends). **Root:** Fuel, carved utensils; natives chewed rootstock for the sweet juice tasting like licorice or boiled and baked them. **Flower:** Woven into garlands. **Architecture:** Motif for temple columns; umbel impressions were used on handles of mirrors and other household furnishings. **Medicinal:** The Ebers papyrus prescribes papyrus in 8 or 9 recipes.

Harvesting and splitting
papyrus.

The Ra Boat. Thor Heyerdahl.
20th Century.

Even in vessels of PAPYRUS upon the waters! Isaiah 18:2

H: Gomeh. F: Papyrus. G: Papyrusgras. I: Papiro.

CULTIVATION
Zones 10–12. Perennial. Will grow in shallow water. Sun.
Propagation by division or seed.

RUSH   Juncus effusus   Butomaceae
Africa, Eurasia

Numerous species of rush grow in Israel's water-ways.
Translators often have difficulty in agreeing which ones apply
to the passage mentioned below.

To 4 feet, bearing soft, pithy,
yellowish-green stems that are
rounded and sheathed with
grasslike leaves. The small flowers
are greenish or brownish.

ANCIENT AND MODERN USES
Stalk: Fodder, mats, chair
bottoms. Marsh tribes still erect
villages on artificial islands built up

on reeds and mud, which are the oldest architectural styles in history. **Pith:** Wicks for oil lamps, tallow candles.

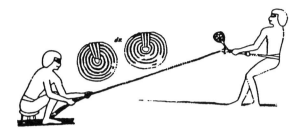

Making ropes. Thebes. 1450 B.C.E.

Can the RUSH shoot up without mire? Can the reed-grass grow without water? Job 8:11

H: Gome, Samar.   F: Jonc.   G: Binse.   I: Giunco.

CULTIVATION
Zones 4–10. Perennial. Moist, heavy clay soil. Propagation by division.

W ATER LILY   Nymphaea alba   Nymphaeaceae
East Africa

Although water lilies are not mentioned by name in the Bible, it is believed that the flowers inspired the architecture of Solomon's Temple. Although the flowers did not grow in Judea, the Israelite carpenters would have seen them in Egypt.

Floating dark-green leaves and fragrant, semi-double white flowers

4–8 inches wide. The plants spread to 10 feet and a clump can cover a small pond.

ANCIENT AND MODERN USES
Seed: Food: Ground into flour, roasted. **Root:** Boiled before consumption. Tanning. **Flowers:** Worn in women's headdress. **Medicinal:** Aphrodiasiac, astringent, narcotic, sedative.

And the capitals that were upon the top of the pillars in the porch were of LILY-WORK.... I Kings: 7:22

H: Shushan.   F: Nenuphar.   G: Seerose.   I. Ninfea.

CULTIVATION
Zones 6–10. Deciduous. Tuber like rhizomes. Require a warm, sunny situation. Propagation by division of rhizomes.

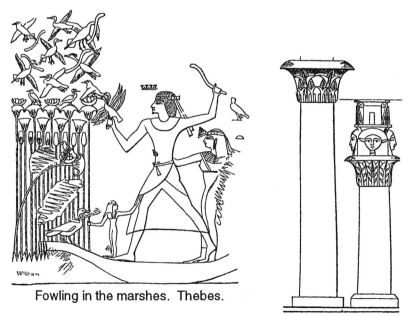

Fowling in the marshes. Thebes.

Lotus and papyrus used as models for columns at Karnak.

SOURCES FOR PLANTS

SEEDS AND HERB PLANTS

Companion Plants. 7247, N. Coolville Ridge Road, Athens, OH 45701. Tel: 614- 592-4643

Richters Herbs. Goodwood, Ontario, LOC 1A0, Canada. Tel: 905-640-6677

Lamb Nurseries. Rt. 1, Box 460B, Long Beach, WA 98631. Tel: 360-642-4856

Well-Sweep Herb Farm. 205 Mt. Bethel Road, Port Murray, NJ 07856. Tel: 908-852-5390

Goodwin Creek Gardens. P.O.Box 83, Williams, OR 97544. Tel: 541-846-7357

Thompson & Morgan. P.O. Box 1308, Jackson, NJ 08527-0308. Tel: 800-274-7333

J. L. Hudson, Seedsman. Star Route 2, Box 337, La Honda, CA 904020. No telephone orders.

Nichols Garden Nursery. 1190 Old Salem Road NE, Albany, OR 97321. Tel: 1-800-422-3985

Territorial Seed Company. P.O. Box 158, Cottage Grove, OR 97424. Tel: 541-942-9547

Select Seeds. 180, Stickney Hill Road, Union, CT 06076. Tel: 1-860-684-9310

Park Seed. 1 Parkton Avenue, Greenwood, S. C. 29647. Tel: 1-800-845-3369

Capriland's Herb Farm. Silver Street, Coventry, CT 06238. Tel: 203-742-7244

Seeds of Change. P.O.B. 15700, Santa Fe, N.M. 87506. Tel: 1-888-762-7333

GRASSES

Kurt Bluemel, Inc. 2740 Greene Lane, Baldwin, MA 21013-9523. Tel: 410-557-7229

Limerock Ornamental Grasses, Inc. R.D. 1 Box 111-C, Port Matilda, PA 16870. Tel: 814-692-2272

TROPICAL AND TEMPERATE PLANTS INCLUDING TREES

Forest Farm. 990 Tetherow Rd. Williams, OR 97544-9599. Tel: 541-846-7269

Glasshouse Works. Church Street, P.O. Box 97, Stewart, OH 45778-0097. Tel: 614-682-2142

Logee's Greeenhouses. 141, North Street, Danielson, CT 06239 - 1939. Tel: 1-888-330-8038

Stokes Tropicals. P.O.Box 9868, New Iberia, LA 70562. Tel: 1-800-624-9706

Pacific Tree Farms. 4301 Lynwood Drive, Chula Vista, CA 92010. Tel: 619-422-2400

Inter-State Nurseries. 1800 Hamilton Road, Bloomington, ILL 61704.

Stark Bro's. P.O. Box 1800, Louisiana, MS 63353. Tel: 1-800-325-4180

Singing Springs Nursery. 8802, Wilkerson Road, Cedar Grove, N. C. 27231. Tel: 919-732-9403

Trans Pacific Nursery. 16065, Oldsville Road, McMinnville, OR 97128. Tel: 503-472-6215

Stallings Exotic Nursery. 910, Encinitas Boulevard, Encinitas, CA 92024. Tel: 619-753-3079

Just Fruits. Route 2, Box 4818, Crawfordville, FL 32327. Tel: 904-926-5644

WATER PLANTS

Paradise Water Gardens. 14 May Street, Whitman, MAS 02382. Tel: 617-447-4711

Van Ness Water Gardens. 2460 North Euclid Avenue, Upland, CA 91786-1199. Tel: 714-982-2425

William Tricker, Inc. 7125 Tanglewood Drive, Independence, OH 44131. Tel: 1-800-524-3492

Lilypons Water Gardens. 6800 Lilypons Road, P.O.Box 10, Buckeystown, MA 21717-0010. Tel: 1-800-999-5459

Slocum Water Gardens. 1101 Cypress Garden Road, Winter Haven, FL 33880. Tel:

BULBS

Brent and Becky's Bulbs. 7463 Heath Trail, Gloucester, VIR 23061. Tel: 877-661-2852

Van Engelen Inc. 23, Tulip Drive, Bantam, CT 06750. Tel: 860-567-8734

White Flower Farm. P.O.Box 50, Litchfield, CT 06759. Tel: 1-800-503-0050

John Scheepers, Inc. 23, Tulip Drive, Bantam, CT 06750-1631. Tel: 860-567-0838

K. Van Bourgondien and Sons. 245 Route 109, P.O. Box 1000, Babylon, N.Y. 11702-9004. Tel: 1-800-552-9996

McClure & Zimmerman. 335 S. High Street, Randolph, WI. 53956. Tel: 1-800-883-6998

Dutch Gardens. P.O. Box 2037, Lakewood, N J 08701. Tel: 1-800-818-3861

Anderson, A.W. *Plants of the Bible.* Philosophical Library Inc., New York, 1957.

Avrin, L. *Scribes, Script and Books. The Book Arts from Antiquity to the Renaissance.* The British Library, London, 1990.

Bailey, C. and A. Danin *Bedouin Plant Utilization in Sinai and the Negev.* Economic Botany Vol.35 (2).

Bauman, B.B. *The Botanical Aspects of Ancient Egyptian Embalming and Burial.* Economic Botany. Vol.14.

Brewer, D.J.and D.B.Redford and S. Redford *Domestic Plants and Animals, The Egyptian Origins.* Aris & Phillips Ltd., Warminster, England. No publication date.

Dalman, G. *Arbeit und Sitte in Palästina.* 7 Vols. Bertelsmann, Gütersloh, 1932.

Dayagi - Mendels, M. *Perfumes and Cosmetics in the Ancient World.* The Israel Museum, Jerusalem, 1989.

De Waal, M. *Medicinal Herbs in the Bible.* Samuel Weiser, Inc., Maine, 1980.

Dittmar, J. *Blumen und Blumensträusse als Opfergabe im alten Ägypten.* Deutscher Kunstverlag, Munich, Berlin, 1986.

Donkin, R.A. *Manna: An Historical Geography.* Dr. W. Junk B.V. Publishers, The Hague-Boston-London, 1980.

Duke, J.A. *Medicinal Plants of the Bible.* Trado-Medic Books, New York, 1983.

Duschak, M. *Botanik des Talmud.* Pest, 1870.

Feinbrun, N. and R. Koppel *Wild Plants in the Land of Israel.* Hakibbutz Hameuchad, Israel, 1960.

Forbes, R.J. *Studies in Ancient Technology.* 9 vol. Brill, Leiden, 1964.

Germer, R. *Flora des pharaonischen Ägypten.* Verlag Philipp von Zabern, Mainz am Rhein, 1985.

Die Pflanzenmaterialien aus dem Grab des Tutanchamun. Gerstenberg Verlag, Hildesheim, 1989.

Die Pflanzen des Alten Ägypten. Verlag Botanisches Museum, Berlin-Dahlem, 1986.

Untersuchung über Arzneimittelpflanzen im Alten Ägypten. Hamburg, 1979.

Goor, A. and M. Nurock *The Fruits of the Holy Land.* Israel Universities Press, Jerusalem, 1968.

Groom, N. *Frankincense and Myrrh.* Longmans, London, New York, 1981.

Guest, E. and Al-Rawi, A. *Flora of Iraq.* 9 Vols. Ministry of Agriculture, Iraq, 1966.

Hareuveni, Nogah. *Tree and Shrub in our Biblical Heritage.* Neot Kedumum, Kiryat Ono, Israel, 1984.

The Emblem of the State of Israel. Neot Kedumim, Israel, 1988.

Ecology in the Bible. Neot Kedumim, Israel, 1974.

Nature in Our Biblical Heritage. Neot   Kedumim, Israel, 1980.

Harrison, R.H. *Healing Herbs of the Bible.* Brill, Leiden, 1966.

Hepper, F.N. *Bible Plants at Kew.* HMSO, London, 1981.

Planting a Bible Garden. Royal Botanic Garden, Kew, London, 1987.

Pharaoh's Flowers. HMSO, London, 1990.

Hunter, D. *Papermaking. The History and Technique of an Ancient Craft.* Alfred A. Knopf, Inc., New York, 1970.

Jacob I. and W. *The Healing Past. Pharmaceuticals in the Biblical and Rabbinic World.* E.J. Brill, Leiden, 1993.

Keimer, L. *Die Gartenpflanzen im alten Ägypten.* Vols. 1 and 2., Verlag Philipp von Zabern, Mainz am Rhein, 1967 and 1984.

King, E.A. *Bible Plants for American Gardens.* Macmillan Co., New York, 1941.

Leach, H.M. *On the Origins of Kitchen Gardening in the Ancient Near East.* University of Otago, Dunedin, New Zealand. No publication date.

Lewis, N. *Papyrus in Classical Antiquity.* Clarendon Press, Oxford, 1974.

Löw, I. *Die Flora der Juden.* 4 Vols., G.O. Hildesheim, 1928

Lucas, A. (rev. by J.R. Harris) *Ancient Egyptian Materials and Industries.* Histories & Mysteries of Man Ltd., London, 1989.

Macht, D. *The Holy Incense.* Baltimore, 1928.

Manniche, L. *An Ancient Egyptian Herbal.* British Museum Publications Ltd., London, 1989.

Martinetz, D. and K. Lohs and J. Janzen *Weihrauch und Myrrhe.* Wisssenschaftlliche Verlagsgesellschaft, Stuttgart, 1988.

Meiggs, R. *Trees and Timber in the Ancient Mediterranean World.* Clarendon Press, Oxford, 1982.

Moldenke, H.N. and A.L. *Plants of the Bible.* Ronald Press Co., New York, 1952.

Morton, J.F. *Major Medicinal Plants.* C. C. Thomas, Springfield, Illinois, 1977.

Nielsen, K. *Incense in Ancient Israel.* Brill, Leiden, 1986.

Parkinson R. and S. Quirke *Papyrus.* British Museum, London, 1995.

Paterson, W. *A Fountain of Gardens.* The Overlook Press, Woodstock, New York, 1990.

Paz, U. *Wild Flowers of the Holyland.* Chartwell Books, Inc., New Jersey, 1979.

Rahn, J.E. *More Plants that Changed History.* Atheneum, New York, 1985.

St. Barbe Baker, R. *Famous Trees of Bible Lands.* H.H.
Greaves Ltd, London, 1974.

Shewell-Cooper, W.E. *God Planted a Garden. Horticulture
in the Bible.* A. James Ltd., Worcs., England, 1977.

Schlott, A. *Schrift und Schreiber im Alten Ägypten.* Beck,
Munich, 1989.

Schoske, K. and R. Germer *"Anch" Blumen für das Leben.*
Munich, 1962.

Smith, W.S. *Animals, Birds and Plants of the Bible.* Hodder
& Stoughton, London, Sydney, Auckland, Toronto. 1971.

United Bible Societies, *Fauna and Flora of the Bible.*
London, 1972.

Uphof, J.C. Th. *Dictionary of Economic Plants.* Verlag von J.
Cramer, Lehre. 1968.

Watt, Sir G. *The Commercial Products of India.* Today &
Tomorrow's Printers & Publishers. New Delhi. Reprint 1966.

Täckholm, V. and M. Drar *Flora of Egypt.* 4 Vols. Reprint.
Otto Koeltz, Koenigstein, 1973.

Waisel, Y. and A. Alon *Trees of the Land of Israel.* Tel
Baruch, Tel Aviv, 1980.

Walker, W. *All the Plants of the Bible.* Doubleday & Co.,
New York, 1979.

Weitz, J. *Forests and Afforestation in Israel.* Massada
Press, Jerusalem, 1974.

Woenig, F. *Die Pflanzen im Alten Aegypten.* Philo Press, Amsterdam, 1971.

Zohary, M. *Plants of the Bible.* Cambridge University Press, Cambridge,1982.

Zohary, D. and M. Hopf *Domestication of Plants in the Old World.* Clarendon Press, Oxford, 1993.

Zohary, M., and N. Feinbrun-Dothan *Flora Palaestina,* 8 Vols., Israel Academy of Science, Jerusalem, 1966–1986.

INDEX

IRENE JACOB

Irene Jacob is the founding director of the Rodef Shalom Biblical Botanical Garden, Pittsburgh, Pennsylvania. Each season she has developed a new program around a theme of ancient horticulture with different plantings, lectures, and exhibits. Through these efforts the garden has developed into an educational vehicle for life in the ancient Near East.

Irene Jacob was educated in Great Britain, Israel, and the United States. She has taught Economic Botany at Chatham College, taught at Phipps Conservatory and initiated its docent program. She has lectured extensively.

Irene Jacob is the author or co-author of *Botanical Symbols in World Religions, The Healing Past*, "Flora" *The Anchor Bible Dictionary, A Guide to the Rodef Shalom Biblical Botanical Garden, Forgotten Immigrants, Gardens of North America and Hawaii.*